THE BOOK OF AMERSHAM

COVER: Amersham in 1818, from an
aquatint by D. Havell, drawn by
L. Hassell. (County Record Office.)

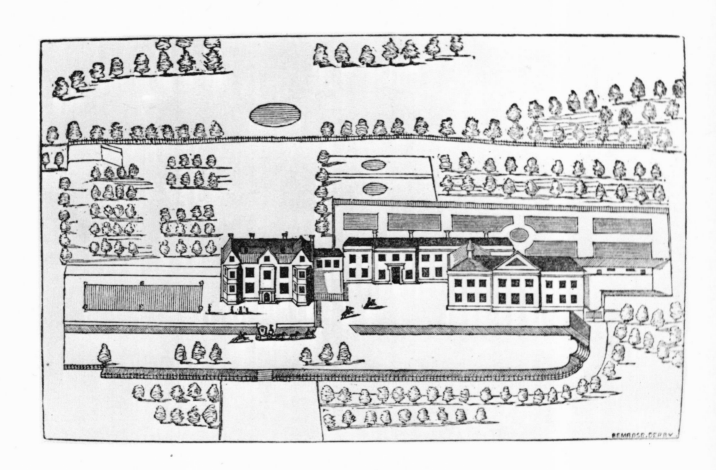

The old mansion at Shardeloes before the present house
was built—from an early print.

THE BOOK OF AMERSHAM

THE STORY OF A CHILTERN TOWN

BY

L. ELGAR PIKE and CLIVE BIRCH

BARRACUDA BOOKS LIMITED
CHESHAM, BUCKINGHAMSHIRE, ENGLAND
MCMLXXVI

PUBLISHED BY BARRACUDA BOOKS LIMITED

CHESHAM, ENGLAND

AND PRINTED BY

FRANK ROOK LIMITED

TOWER BRIDGE ROAD

LONDON SE I

BOUND BY

BOOKBINDERS OF LONDON LIMITED

LONDON N5

JACKET PRINTED BY

WHITE CRESCENT PRESS LIMITED

LUTON, ENGLAND

LITHOGRAPHY BY

SOUTH MIDLANDS LITHO PLATES LIMITED

LUTON, ENGLAND

TYPE SET IN

MONOTYPE BASKERVILLE SERIES 169

BY SOUTH BUCKS TYPESETTERS LIMITED

BEACONSFIELD, ENGLAND

ISBN 0 86023 028 7

Contents

Acknowledgements

Our thanks as joint authors go to a wide variety of people and organisations, for help with information and illustrations, and in particular to John Armistead for devoting many hours and much skill to the reproduction of all but a handful of the pictures in this book. He has developed old negatives, travelled outside Amersham on our behalf, and spent many days in the town itself, working on location shots and within people's homes to provide the abundance of material from which we have selected merely a fifth, for publication.

We are grateful also to Chris Gowing and Rosemary Ewles of the County Museum, especially to Rosemary for turning up material at short notice, to Hugh Handley at the County Record Office for his advice, and his help in locating archive material, and to County Librarian Colin Rippon and his staff at Amersham, Chesham and Little Chalfont Libraries, and also Amersham sub-post office for their assistance with the subscription lists. A special debt is owed to Gerald and Elizabeth Elvey for providing and annotating archive material in the care of the Buckinghamshire Archaeological Society.

Many others have helped, including Amersham Town Council, Chiltern District Council, Lady Swiney, Brig E. E. F. Baker, Rev A. Campbell, Misses Baker, T. Boughton, Mrs C. M. Brown, L. A. Haddon, E. Hearne, H. R. Hoare, J. Keen, F. W. E. King, A. Mead, Mrs Patterson, Mrs F. Payne, E. Pugh, J. Reading, W. Reynolds, A. G. Shrimpton, W. H. Smith, A. T. Sykes, Mrs B. Thomas, A. R. Woodley, J. Hearn, P. F. Marson, and Bert Flack. Dr Denis Rhodes, Assistant Keeper of Printed Books, British Library was instrumental in defining the Totell role in Amersham, and Ron White lent us a rare and magnificent collection of George Ward negatives. Tony White and Bernard Edwards of the *Bucks Examiner* and the *Bucks Advertiser* have taken a positive interest in this book, and both Earl Howe and Brigadier Baker have been kind enough to contribute their comments on the opposite page. Lastly, both our wives have earnt our gratitude for their sympathetic response to the pressures of authorship.

Dedication

For the people of Amersham

8

Foreword

by The Rt. Hon. The Earl Howe, CBE, DL

I am very pleased to be given the opportunity to contribute a brief foreword for this story of the town.

Within 25 miles of London lies Agmondesham, known to everyone today as Amersham. This old market town has so much to commend it: the High Street with its fine old houses of so many periods, the little courtyards leading to picturesque homes, almshouses and inns, the ancient market hall in the middle of High Street and dating to 1682, when it was built by Sir William Drake. One of the most striking features of the town must be this wide main street, which in its design and beauty must be hard to equal anywhere.

Unfortunately, some of the peaceful serenity of the old town is spoilt today by the ever-increasing traffic flow, but this is a national problem of our times, which will be solved.

I am sure that the authors of this book will have found their subject of absorbing interest. Research into Amersham's past brings to light so much that has been forgotten as the years roll by. The Book of Amersham merits success.

PENN HOUSE,
AMERSHAM.
November 1976.

Howe.

Preface

by Brig E. E. F. Baker, CB, CBE, DSO, MC

Less than fifty years ago there were occasions when I had to chase cows out of my garden at Oakfield Corner. Our dog would sit in the middle of the crossroads almost with impunity. At night, walking up Hill Avenue, one could fill one's shoes with muddy water; it was better to wear gumboots. The only building nearby was the Station Hotel.

Then, there were three houses on the north side of Sycamore Road, but none on the south side—just a grass verge, hedgerow and some trees. A few shops clustered round Oakfield Corner, designated New Town on the ordnance map.

Today this is Amersham-on-the-Hill, and part of the history of the town told here in this fascinating book. The authors are well known for their interest in and careful research into local history. We should be grateful to them for presenting the result of their labours in such eminently attractive form.

OAKFIELD CORNER,
AMERSHAM.
November 1976.

Euston Baker

Amersham Bells

I likes to hear the huntsman's cry, the sound of horn and beagle,
I loves to hear 'em playing at quoits at the back of the good old Eagle;
'Tis pleasant enough, come harvest time, to hear 'em cuttin' the wheat,
And they little 'ole crickets 'll cheer you up, if ye're out by night in the street;
We've many good songs and sounds and cries, but there's one that far excells,
For what we Amersham folks likes best is the sound of Amersham Bells.

There's old Town Crier, he rings his bell, and he makes you fairly smile
With his funny 'O yes!' and 'God save the King' in his extry-martial style;
There's the bell that rings on Market Day,—though I don't know what it's about—
There's the Fire Bell too,—that's what they rings, when they wants the moon put out!
But it isn't they bells at all I mean, as ye might have guessed before,
No! It's them that's hung for hundreds of year in Amersham old Church tower!

It weren't plain sailing all the way when I was courting Sal,
For I was a hot-headed sort of chap, and she was a peppery gal!
And things kept going from bad to worse until—I can't tell how—
One day we fell to 't, hammer and tongs, in a regular right-down row.
I says: 'I'm going for over-seas!' Says she: 'And welcome, too!'
If there weren't another in Amersham Town, I wouldn't be seen with *you*!'

She turns her back, and I turns mine—I *were* in a nasty mood!—
We was leaning together across the gate up there in Rectory Wood—
'Good-bye!' I says, and I leaps the style, and off and away to go,
When all of a sudden the sound o' bells came clashing up from below;
'Jingle—jangle!' 'Ding—ding—dong!' my word, but they knocked me flat!
'Go back!' they rang, 'Go back, you fool! don't leave your girl like that!'

Well, Amersham Bells had done the trick—they'd sort 'o cleared the air,—
And there was Sally and me again, a regular pigeon-pair!
So right in the middle of Tenter Field (there weren't none there to see)!
We catches hands and we dances round like kiddies out for a spree!
And I takes her into my arms and says: 'If so be you'll agree,
'Fore ever it comes to harvest moon, 'twill be Amersham Bells for we!'

PAUL ENGLAND.
c. 1916

Hagmondesham

'Hagmondesham, alias Hamersham, a right praty market towne on Friday of on strete well buildyd with tymbar, standynge in Bukinghamshire and Chiltern'. Although it was some four and a half centuries ago when John Leland, topographer to Henry VIII, journeyed through Amersham and so recorded it, this venerable and historic town still, to a great degree, conforms to this description.

Originally two Romano-British farming settlements, later the 'ham' or homestead of a Saxon family, then a royal Saxon manor given by William the Conqueror to Geoffrey de Mandeville, Constable of the Tower of London, granted a charter by King John in the year 1200 for a weekly market and an annual fair, returning two members to Parliament as a pocket borough up to the Reform Act of 1832 ... Amersham may well be said to represent, by its records and its community life, a truly miniature history of England.

The town has witnessed that pageant of English history down the centuries. Gore Hill has been the focus of residents' attention, just as Station Road has divided them. Tradition holds that on that bloody hill the Danes fought the Saxons; from that vantage point Amersham people gazed in wonder at the night-sky reflection of London's Great Fire of 1666, and a mere three-plus decades ago, they stared again at that same night sky as London suffered the incendiary onslaught of the blitz.

Amersham is now two communities within one, with a third satellite community at Little Chalfont, and its long lived neighbours at Woodrow, Winchmore Hill, Coleshill and Chesham Bois. Today, Amersham on the Hill is home to many newcomers as well as established families. Amersham Town has embraced the wealthy, the eccentric and the perpetual visitor. Yet Leland's description still holds good for the heart of the community, and this is the story of that Chiltern town, spanning nearly two thousand years—the living history of Amersham.

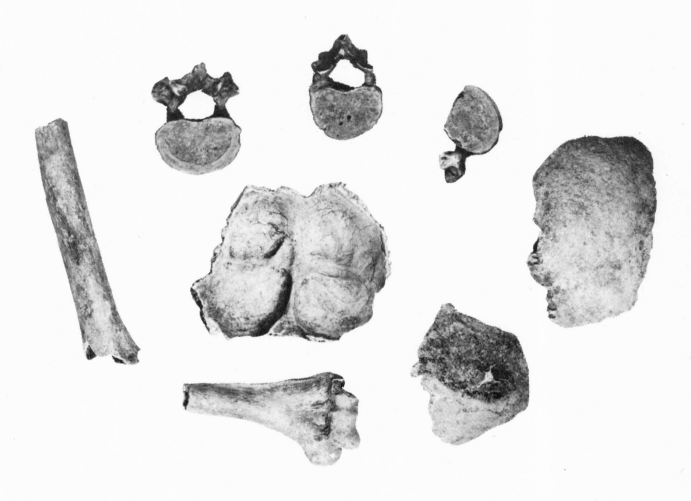

ABOVE: Some 3,500 years ago Bronze Age man dropped his spear in the Misbourne; the spearhead survived. (County Museum)

BELOW: Amersham's first residents: these Romano-British 4th century remains were found at Mantles Green Farm.

Early Imprints

Amersham lies within one of the few watered valleys running off the Chiltern heights down to the Burnham plateau, where the only favourable areas for permanent settlement were the banks of the Chess, the Alder Bourne and the Misbourne. The series of weaving tracks, which together made up the ancient Icknield Way across the Chiltern Ridge, left these and their companion valleys on this side of the hills an isolated island in earliest times.

A prehistoric trackway, which was probably a trade route, came southwards past Chesham at Ley Hill, down across the Chess, up the significantly named Hollow Way Lane and Bois Lane in Chesham Bois and over the extensive common to Amersham. From there it continued past the equally significantly named Coldharbour Farm at Coleshill, on through Beaconsfield and possibly along Pybush and Burtley Lanes and Hollow Way to a ford over the Thames.

Such routes are marked by distinctive boulders of rock called conglomerates. These were either of pebbles in a stonelike matrix (popularly called pudding stones) or sarsens of sandstone. A number of the former, presumably from the route through Chesham Bois but now broken up, can be seen lining the drive from Bois Lane to The Warren and Chesham Bois House. Others of sandstone are in The Broadway, Church Street and other places in Amersham. One in Back Lane, opposite Mill Lane, may well mark the route of another branch of this prehistoric trackway.

Early (Palaeolithic) man passed nearby, 250,000 and more years ago, leaving traces of his wandering at both Missendens and Chalfont St Giles; he touched on Chesham too. So did Middle Stone Age (Mesolithic) Man, ten thousand years ago. New Stone Age (Neolithic) Man was in the area four thousand years later, and left more evidence in more places.

The only tangible evidence of far-off days is a Bronze Age looped spearhead (now in the County Museum) which was found in the River Misbourne near the bottom of Station Road in 1956. This must have been either dropped or discarded by a nomadic hunter who was passing this way about 3,500 years ago. Beyond this, nothing has so far been found in Amersham of prehistoric times although the later Iron Age people had a camp or settlement at Cholesbury.

Later still, when the inhabitants had settled down under Roman rule, a number of thriving Romano-British farming communities were established in this part of the Chilterns. The one at Latimer is well known, and others existed in Chesham, Chenies and Sarratt. When the road out of Amersham to Aylesbury was straightened and widened in 1955, the bulldozers turned up Roman brickwork, masses of broken pottery including Samian ware, and some glass fragments, as well as numerous coins, which dated these remnants to the 4th century AD. The actual site of what was obviously a Romano-British farming community has not yet been accurately located; presumably it lies somewhere beneath this main road. It is significant that it is close to a former farmhouse called Coldmoreham. As

13

with Coldharbour Farm at Coleshill, names including the word 'cold' are invariably adjacent to Roman or prehistoric sites.

In 1965, workmen erecting electricity poles from near Coldmoreham to Mantles Green Farm, dug up numerous human bones, including three skulls. These were nearly two thousand years old, and therefore of the same period as the 1955 finds. So these were the bones (now in the County Museum) of the first people to live in Amersham.

There was another similar Romano-British farming community less than a mile away, just beyond Chequers Hill. This was discovered in 1972. Unfortunately the site must have been previously disturbed, but foundation walls were excavated, and Roman pottery and other contemporary remains found. Earlier, in 1964, Roman pottery was dug up in the new Amersham cemetery on Stanley Hill; and in 1957 some 4th century Roman coins and pottery were found during the building of Stevens House in Whielden Street. All this shows that some 1,700 years ago Amersham had a well established farming life. Although some of the glass fragments recovered from the Coldmoreham site were of the 4th century, others have been identified as Saxon, including part of a beaker, confirming that this place was inhabited both in Roman and Saxon times.

Various roads of the Roman period have been traced around Amersham, mainly local roads linking the various farming communities or so-called villas. One came diagonally up the hillside from the Latimer villa, past Raans Farm and on an almost undeviating course down Raans Road to Blackhorse Bridge, over Stanley Hill and halfway along the modern Stanley Hill Avenue. Where this residential road bears right, the Roman route continued straight down what has now become a public footpath to Station Road, then over this and up the opposite side, (still marked by a present-day footpath) into Amersham. Here it went up Whielden Street to reach the large Roman settlement at The Rye, High Wycombe, with a branch off to Coldmoreham.

The most important Roman road, which was only discovered by aerial survey in 1955, linked the two great road junctions of Verulamium (St Albans) and Silchester in Hampshire. Coming up North Lane at Chorleywood, close by the county border, it ran in a straight line to The Vache at Chalfont St Giles, then on through Malthouse Square in Beaconsfield, to ford the Thames near Hedsor.

LEFT: An ancient sarsen still in The Broadway, by the gasworks gate.

RIGHT: Roman coins that surfaced at Coldmoreham, LEFT: Claudius II Gothicus 270 AD; CENTRE: Constantine I's son 337-341 AD; RIGHT: Gratianus 367-375 AD.

ABOVE: The Romans imported pottery and made their own: these sherds (above) are from native made pots; the other two (below) are Samian ware

BELOW: This was once part of the floor of Amersham's Roman Villa.

6 TERRA GOZELINI BRITONIS. In Burneha hund'.

1 Gozelinus Brito ten' In Elmodesham dim' hid. Tra e .i. car. 7 ibi e cu .v. bord. 7 i. molin de .iiii. sol. pau .i. car. Val 7 ualuit sep .xx. sol. hanc tra tenuit Aluric ho Godric uicecom'. 7 uende pot. In Coteslai hd.

2 In Elmodesha ten' Almar de com'. In Burnehu hd. dim' hid. Tra e .ii. car. 7 ibi sunt cu .i. uillo 7 i. bord. pau .ii. car. Silua .xx. porc. Val 7 ualuit sep .xx. sol. hanc tra tenuit Siuuard ho Aldene. 7 potuit uende.

3 In Elmodesha ten' Rogeri de epo dim' hid. Tra e .i. car. 7 ibi e cu .iii. bord. 7 i. molin de .iiii. sol. pau .i. car. h tra ual 7 ualuit sep .xx. sol. hanc tenuit tra Aluuin ho regine Eddid. 7 uendere potuit.

4 In Elmodesha ten' Vluiet de hugone In Burneha hd. dimid hid. Tra e .ii. car. 7 ibi sunt cu .ii. uillis 7 iii. bord. Ibi .i. molin de .v. sol. Silua .xx. porc. Val 7 ualuit sep .xx. sol. Iste met tenuit T.R.E. 7 uende potuit.

5 In Elmodesha ten' Turstin dim' hid. Tra e .ii. car. Ibi est una. 7 alia pot fieri. Ibi .ii. uilli cu uno bord. pot .ii. car. Silua .xxx. porc. Val 7 ualuit .xiii. sol 7 iiii. den. T.R.E. .xx. sol. hanc tra tenuit Turchil ho R.E.

Seven tenants held from their lord controlling interests in Amersham; the Domesday Survey of 1086 details the administrative areas involved and the men themselves. 1. Gozelin the Breton held about 60 acres including a mill; 2. Almar held the same with ploughlands for two teams and woodland sufficient to feed 20 swine; 3. Roger's holding was the same size, with one plough team and a mill; 4. Ulviet held the same area, with land for two ploughs, and a mill; his woodland fed 20 swine; 5. Turstin also held 60 acres, but he only had one plough team when there was scope for two; his woods fed 30 swine.

Men of Manors

Probably the earliest charter concerning Amersham refers to a grant of land here by Berhtric, king of the West Saxons, dated AD 796. The name Ealhmund appears in this document and provides a clue to the origin of the place name: Ealgmund's ham or homestead. In 1066, on his deathbed, Edward the Confessor dedicated land in various places to his monastic foundation of the 'West Minster' (Westminster Abbey). This charter, marked with the royal cross included land at 'Agmodesham and Wedon', although at that time the former was in fact owned by Queen Edith. Wedon comprised an area between Amersham and Little Missenden which was later entered in the Domesday Survey as owned by the Count of Mortain and Hugh de Bolbec. Subsequently known as the manor of Wedon Hill, this was the subject of a legal dispute in 1601, when the rights of the Count's descendants were represented in court by the Honour of Berkhamsted. Wedon is derived from the Old English 'weo-dun', meaning a hilly place with a heathen temple.

Amersham is defined by the Domesday Survey of 1086 as an area of 10 hides (one hide equals 120 acres), divided between the Bishop of Bayeux, the Count of Mortain, Geoffrey de Mandeville, Hugh de Bolbec, Turstin Mantel and Gozelin the Breton.

The fact that there were far fewer plough teams recorded for this district (and, in fact, for all the Chilterns) than in the north of the county, indicates that it was even then a well wooded area. Domesday confirms the extensive local woodlands.

The principal manor of Amersham remained with the Earldom of Essex until the 14th century (with a re-grant of the title in 1199 when the original Mandeville family line died out and the estates passed to in-laws). Amersham was then possessed by the Earls of Northampton who in 1421 assigned it to the Countess of Stafford, and she to her son who was created Duke of Buckingham in 1444. A personal letter written by Richard III to Henry Stafford, Duke of Buckingham, denouncing him for his traitorous conduct in raising a rebellion in Wales, resulted in his execution in 1483 when his estates were forfeit to the Crown. After a grant of a life tenancy to one, Thomas Fowler, Amersham was returned to the disgraced Duke's son Edward; in 1521 he was attainted for high treason and beheaded.

By 1526 the Russell family of Chenies, already owning considerable local property, added to it the manor of Amersham; but in 1637 they disposed of this to the Drakes of Shardeloes whose successors, the Tyrwhitt Drakes, have retained the lordship ever since, although they sold off much of the town in 1928 and subsequently their historic seat of Shardeloes and most of their other local holdings.

In early times Shardeloes itself was a separate manor, owned in the 13th century by the notable de Bohun family. The estate appears to have derived its name from Adam de Shardeloes, to whom it was granted in 1308. Passing quickly through various hands, it was acquired by the Brudenell family of Raans in 1406, and conveyed in 1479 to Thomas Cheyne, of the Chesham Bois family which held it until 1596, when it was purchased by William

Tothill, a lawyer and one of the Six Clerks in Chancery, who had altogether 33 children but no male heir. So it passed by the marriage of his eldest daughter, Joane, to Francis Drake of Esher who was a Gentleman of the Privy Chamber. Although not related to the famous Sir Francis, the Drakes came from the same stock as the great Duke of Marlborough, both being descended from the Drakes of Ashe in Devonshire. The eminence and wealth of the Shardeloes family in the 16th century can be gathered from the statement that 'Mr William Drake may be esteemed one of the wealthiest Commoners in England'.

The Amersham Drakes liked to think they were related to their celebrated namesake. That Drake was said to have axed his cabin boy to death for knowing too much about matters nautical. Elizabeth I therefore decreed that all Drake carriages should have blood-red wheels as a mark of dishonour, and the family crest be surmounted by a blood-stained axe. All the carriages ever used by the Amersham Drakes displayed scarlet painted wheels. Even when they changed to motorcars in the 1920s, their wheels carried a blood red circle apiece. Predictably, their coat-of-arms incorporates a blood stained axe, although Robert the Bruce is said to have cleft the skull of a Drake with his battle axe, and perhaps the family remembered this bloody act by way of their crest.

Earlier, William Tothill's (Totell's) father, Richard, came to London from Exeter and set up as a stationer and printer, despite a substantial private income. He became one of the most prosperous and important of the Tudor publishers, largely because he held from Edward VI onwards a royal patent for printing legal books: 'All and almaner bokes of oure Tempall lawe called the comon lawe whatsoever they be'. He also produced 'Tottell's Miscellany'. This was a collection of early Court poetry which went into six editions and most of the Elizabethan poets were 'brought up on it'.

He devoted some of his wealth to the acquisition of land in his home county of Devon, and in Buckinghamshire, probably because he was related to the already established Cheynes of Chesham Bois. In 1572 he bought a farm at Little Missenden, several hundred acres two years later at Wendover, an estate at 'Bukland Chollesbury' and houses and fields at Little Missenden and 'Agmondesham'. In 1575 he purchased from Thomas Sherley the manor of Wedon Hill of over 10,000 acres for £1,120. On his death in 1593 this manor passed to his son, William, and so to the Drakes. It is in part still owned by the Tyrwhitt Drake family.

In 1581, following his father's sound investment example, William had purchased for £100 from his cousin, Sir Henry Cheyne, an estate of some 60 acres, being: 'all those parcells of lande called Pipers' in Amersham and Little Missenden. In 1596, three years after his father's death, he obtained for £400 'all that the Lordshippe and mannor of Agmondesham Woodrowe with all the rights, members and appurtenances thereof'.

Of the other local manors the most important was Raans, originally also granted to the de Mandevilles, Earls of Essex, and tenanted by Jordan de Rane. Later this family acquired the lordship which passed by marriage to the Groves, and then in the 15th century to the Brudenells who held it until 1608. The manor house was largely rebuilt by Sir Peter Proby who held the lordship from 1619. By 1735 Raans had been purchased by the Duke of Bedford for £8,000 to further augment the Russell estates. At the end of the 18th century it was sold to Lord George Cavendish (created Earl of Burlington) whose descendants held it with the barony of Chesham. The small manor of Tomlyns, or Tokeville, was for some three hundred years a possession of the Agmondesham family; but in 1657 this, too, was added to the Drake estate. The separate manor called the Hamlet of Amersham, originally owned also by the de Mandevilles, passed to the Despensers, then to the Dukes of Buckingham, and so to William Tothill and, by marriage, to the Drakes. In due course the Drakes also became possessed of Woodrow and Woodside through the Fleetwoods and Tothill.

Of the surrounding manors, that of Chesham Bois managed to retain its separate identity. Originally a Saxon manor, it was given in 1063 by William the Conqueror to his half-brother Odo, Bishop of Bayeux. Later held by the Honour of Leicester and by the Duchy of Lancaster, it was acquired by the du Bois, or du Boyes, at the beginning of the 13th century, deriving the second part of its name from this family and not, as has so often been assumed, from the fact that it was a well wooded place. By 1446 it had come into the possession of Sir Thomas Cheyne. His family, which had been lords of Isenhampsted Cheyne (now Chenies) in the 12th century, continued to hold Chesham Bois for three hundred years. Charles Cheyne, who was created Viscount Newhaven, had married Lady Jane Cavendish. She came to him with a handsome dowry out of which he purchased the estate of Chelsea where the family name is retained in Cheyne Walk and Cheyne Row. He owned the salmon fishery rights here; also he sold off some of the manor land for the famous physic garden and part of the Hospital of the Chelsea Pensioners. On the death of the widow of William Cheyne, second and last Viscount Newhaven, Chesham Bois passed to a relative, Lord Gower, who disposed of it in 1738 to the acquisitive Duke of Bedford, the Russell family retaining it until 1903.

The other local manor of Stokebury, also known as Braynford (commemorated by the present Brentford Grange), comprised Coleshill and extended down to Bury End in Amersham. After the Conquest it was possessed by the Earls of Essex with the Quarrendon family (still remembered by Quarrendon Farm) occupying it as tenants in the 13th century. They were succeeded by Walter Agmondesham and then by the Brudenells when it became known as Coleshill, the lord of the manor by this time being—who else but—Sir John Russell of Chenies. The Brudenells subsequently obtained the ownership but disposed of it in 1506 to William Counser. He sold it to Edmund Waller, son of the poet, from whom it was purchased by Sir Basil Brook. A later owner was James Perrot, steward and subsequently executor of Sir William Drake, Bart, and probably a relation of Edward Perrot, the prominent Amersham Quaker, whose funeral in 1665 was such a dramatic event in the town. What remained of this manor was finally purchased by the trustees of the will of Elizabeth Bent, a widow of Amersham, to provide a fee for the rector of Amersham 'for ever' for preaching four special sermons every year.

Amersham's main lord in 1086 was Geoffrey de Mandeville. He held Elmodesham itself—an area of 900 acres, with land for sixteen ploughs. The home farm comprised 240 acres worked by three plough teams, 14 villeins and four bordars themselves operating a further nine ploughs. There was room for four more teams. Of serfs there were seven, and the woodlands fed 400 swine.

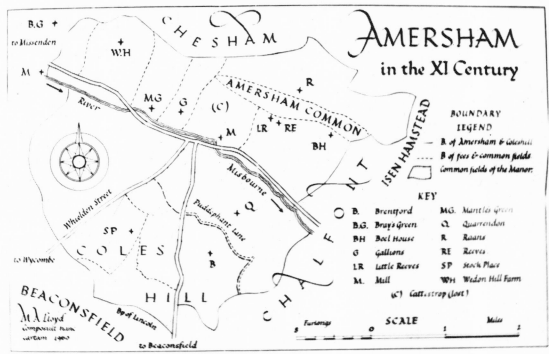

ABOVE: The heraldic devices of Amersham's great families: left to right—
Bohun, Drake, Proby, Mandeville, Stafford, Brudenell, Brewes, Fitz John.

CENTRE: Rarely does Domesday allow us to visualise the actual bounds
of the places involved; Amersham's entries do, and this map shows us
what was where in 1086. (Bucks Archaeological Society)

BELOW LEFT: Russell, first Earl of Bedford; CENTRE: Geoffrey de Mandeville,
Earl of Essex, and RIGHT: Stafford, Duke of Buckingham.
(Mansell Collection)

ABOVE: Raans Farm House at Amersham.

BELOW: Michael Birch collected the quit rents for the lord of the manor of Wedon Hill in 1629—he recorded them all in a notebook. This is the first page. (Bucks Archaeological Society)

21

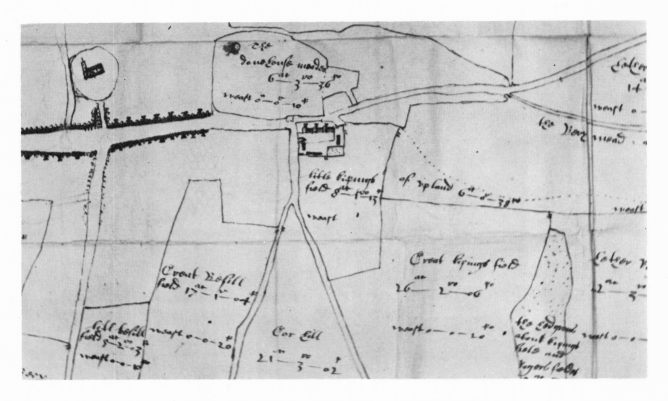

ABOVE: John Halsey drew this map of the Manor
of Amersham in 1637. (Bucks Archaeological Society)

BELOW: William, Earl of Bedford, Lord Russell;
17th century. (Mansell Collection)

Will: Manser Butler came to me Oct yᵉ 9 : 1759
is to have 16 pᵈ year wages & Washen

Deembʳ 1729

Recᵈ then of Mrˢ Drake the Sume off
Sixteen pounds for a years wages Due
the 26 May 1729 Last past
                                    Wᵐ Manser

ABOVE: Little Shardeloes.

BELOW: The butler's writing looks better than that of mistress Drake
when William Manser acknowledged his annual 16 pence wages for the
year, in 1729. (County Record Office)

LEFT: The tax return of 1700 (this is a 1707 copy) detailed the servants at Shardeloes. (County Record Office)

RIGHT: In 1777 these were the land rentals on the Drake estate. (County Record Office)

Prayer and Protest

Geoffrey de Mandeville, grandson of the Geoffrey who accompanied William I, endowed nineteen churches in the 12th century—one of them at Amersham. This is our first evidence of the foundation of St Mary's, though it would be surprising if it was not preceded by a Saxon foundation, and a probably wooden place of worship, just as Chesham's church dates back to the 10th century.

For centuries Amersham served as the centre church for the whole district including Chesham, and as was the custom before the Reformation, parishioners from surrounding places walked in procession to their mother church at Amersham. But the churchmen of the town resented this annual event as an intrusion on their territory by the people of Chesham, for they had never got on well together, particularly in religious matters. This hostile attitude was demonstrated by quarrels and open fighting, with punching and shin kicking and, in the end, the use of clubs and staves.

So the Chesham people petitioned the bishop in far-off Lincoln that they might be allowed to process around their own church with Chesham Bois and Latimer joining them. The bishop, having duly considered the matter, agreed to their request provided that they paid the sum of sixteen pence annually towards the upkeep of Lincoln Cathedral. Since then, of course, the vast diocese of Lincoln has been split up and the whole of Buckinghamshire in now in the diocese of Oxford.

Structurally the parish church of Amersham dates from the 13th to the 15th centuries with the addition of the Drake chapel about two hundred years ago. The fine western tower, embattled and turreted, carries a peal of six bells. As a tablet on the exterior wall records, this tower was rebuilt in 1888 by Thomas Tyrwhitt Drake, who was fortunate enough to obtain the flints to face it at presumably no cost, from the cutting below Longfield Drive when the Metropolitan Railway was extended to Aylesbury. Unusual interior features of this handsome and extremely well restored church are the upper parts of the two original doorways still recessed in the south aisle walls. For, no doubt due to flooding by the Misbourne, which flowed—and still sometimes does—beside the churchyard, the floor had to be raised nearly four feet in the 15th century, and the present doorways made at a higher level. Prior to this it must have been uncomfortable, as no seating was then provided in churches, the people standing or kneeling during what were often long services.

In the neat churchyard there are barrel and cast iron gravestones, and about seventy years ago the Drake burial vault was converted into the present Lady chapel, the coffins re-interred in two long rows in the churchyard on the north side of the church, and marked with oval flat stones showing the names and dates. The pathway here from Church Street to the cemetery became known as Lozenger Avenue, or Peppermint Walk. The stones have been temporarily removed.

It is rare for sixteenth century churchwardens' accounts to survive, due to the wholesale destruction of records by the Tudors, but an 1892 commentator was able to examine

Amersham records dating from 1541 to 1603. These include such entries as 'payd for mendying of ye orgynbellos . . . vij^d' and 'for a bybull . . . ix^s ix^d' as well as 'for fechynge of the bybull . . . iis.' One series of entries gives an idea of the extent of the church property in 1541:

'The bounds of the churche yarde of Agmondysh'm.

Imprimis, the stone wall w'th the gatte & the style towards the streate the hole Towne muste repayre and myteyne.

It'. Wedyn Hill A D'perche now in the Tenure of Thom's Saundr's (Henry Germon).

It'. coperkyng's land a perche now in the Tenure of Chambers and John Gardyner of Ranes. (Robt. Hemphry.)'

And the entries continue like this, mentioning Galyens land, Cook's land, Barn's, John Chylds, Will'm Carter's, Thom's Gardyners, Rayne's and Thom's mylsents' lands, Darby's lond, pyper's lond, Thomas Russell's lands, Rydynge's londs and Colyn's land. Other named properties include those of powtrew, Rare, Cumsutlatt, Stompe, Barrows, Stockton, and Bacheler's.

Later in this document, someone has written 'here was a likely master fooll of supersticion. thi will be done o lord.'

When it came to 'amending of the churche walle by the town' the donations listed vary somewhat. Of 83 'benefactions' Dorsett of the White Harte gave vj^d while Mr Cheny contributed ij^s vj^d.

The earliest records of wax for candles suggests a substantial endowment of plate and other goods. By 1541, the inventory of church goods and chattels is vague, reflecting the rapacity of local men, plundering their own church after the example of their monarchs. Included are the 'best sewte' but not the inferior ones that this implies; five chalices whose metal is not described, thirteen altar cloths, indicating the importance of Amersham church at the time, and no candlesticks—the most suspicious omission, as they are mentioned in the accounts.

By 1603 times had changed, and one startling item in the accounts reflected the considerable consumption of wine at communion.

'Imprimis for one rundlett of wyne . . . xx^s ij^d' and again, 'Item for another rundlett of wine 8g. . . . xxix^s iv^d' and 'Ite' for ij rundletts of wyne x gallons d . . . xxxv^s' and yet more: 'Ite' for one rundlett more x gallons d . . . xxii^s ij^d' plus one splendid addition: 'Ite' for my charges at London when I went to by the wyne . . . xiiij^d.'

Dr F. G. Lee's comment in 1892 cannot be bettered when reading the final inventory for 1603. He said 'Church robbers had evidently been at work.'

That inventory lists 'the church dore key, the communyon cupp, a great peuter pott, a quart pott, a peuter dysh, a herisha cloth, a cloth for the pulpitt, two carpitts for the communio' table, two cloths for the communio' table, a chest, a gable or rowl, a table on a frame, with other descent ornaments belonging to the churche. A byble a bouck of com'an prayers with two other boukes. There remaining at the psn'age x^li of lead.' One wonders what happened to the rest of the lead!

The Churchwardens' and Overseers' Accounts provide both interesting reading and a background to the communal life and happenings in the parish, as a brief selection from the many later entries shows:

1651   Releeved 3 Dutchmen who brought a Certifficate   4d

1653   Recd. of David Salter, Constable, money levied to the Poore's use upon
       two offenders, one for being druncke and the other for swearing   10s 0d

1681	Releeved 3 poore souldiers yt came from Tangier wounded	1s 0d
1682	Cloth to lay over the beare	£3 2s 3d
1683	Katharine Cooke and Mary Greene poor widdows being burnt out	1s 6d
1684	Releeved Thomas Dams and his wife being very sicke	6d
1686	Item recd. of John Young for his father being buried in lynnen	£2 10s 0d
1687	Mrs Mari Lisle with her three children, forsed to flee for there religion from France	2s 0d
1689	Gave to the Ringers for Ringing when King William and Quene Mary was crowned, the sume of	10s 0d
1697	Recd. from the mad woman by a ring and money	10s 0d
1706	To Mr Gefostes of Oxbridge to take Henry Mason apprentis and to cloath him	£6 0s 0d
1707	Pd. Wm. Hollom for Boxing the Widow Gardner	2s 6d
1708	Widdow Watson to pay the pothecary for stuff for her legge	7s 0d
1709	Goody Redding curing Ather's toe	1s 0d
1711	Paid for bleding Eliz. Wood	1s 0d
1717	To a great bellyed woman to gett her out of Towne	3s 0d
1724	Paid Rob Boller for carridge of tow Chardon of Coles from yr Wharf	12s 0d
1794	Paid John Shrimpton of Amersham, Paper maker, with his apprentice Wm. Nevill and part expenses	£5 6s 8d
1800	Paid John Russell of Amersham, Barber, Peruke maker and Hair dresser, with his apprentice Thos. Stevens	£5 4s 2d

The Goodwives, or Goodies, frequently referred to in the parochial accounts were the women who were employed to nurse the sick poor. Examples of reimbursement for expenditure in their work are:—

For nesaries for people not well	2s 3½d
Two yards of Cloath to mend shurts	1s 0d
For children's heads and feate	9d

When, as at Amersham, the squire held the gift of the church living, it was customary for one of the sons, or failing these a relation, to be the rector. For such the Drakes provided in the 17th century a large and handsome Rectory on the hillside above the town as a suitable residence. This still has its old donkey well. The fine stable block beyond has been converted into two private houses and the timber-framed barn is also now a private residence. The upkeep of the Rectory appears to have been somewhat neglected, as we find that the Revd the Hon Henry Brydges (rector 1721-8) became a tenant of the Probys at Raans when the parsonage was in 'poor condition'. The Drakes were a keen hunting family, the famous Old Berkeley kennels being for many years on their estate. Being ordained did not quell their sporting instinct, so frequently the rector could be seen hurrying out of the church to his waiting horse in full hunting pink, which had been barely concealed beneath his ecclesiastical robes during the service.

Although there had long been a chapel-of-ease at Coleshill, it was many years before another one became necessary 'on the common' which developed as Amersham-on-the-Hill. A small church was built there in the early 1920s, with a general purpose hall in front of it on Sycamore Road. This has now given place to a modern complex of church, hall, ancillary accommodation, vicarage and car park, and Amersham-on-the-Hill has become a separate parish.

A corrugated iron building for church services was also erected at the junction of Stanley

Hill and White Lion Road; designated St Mary's Mission Church, it was locally known as the Tin Tabernacle. This was subsequently removed after St George's, built near Bell Lane in 1935, had replaced it; but there was a long delay before the surviving trustees could be found to give their consent to the clearing away of the disused temporary building.

Nonconformity had always been strong in Amersham with its history of steadfastness against persecution, as displayed by the Lollard martyrs of the 15th and 16th centuries, and by the Quakers who regularly suffered imprisonment during the 17th century.

There is a Meeting House of the Society of Friends in Whielden Street which, according to Quaker records, was first leased in 1627. The membership later fell away and it was closed in 1850. On a map of 1882 it is shown as a Wesleyan chapel, but it was re-opened by the Society of Friends in 1917. The present Wesleyan Chapel (Methodist) stands at the west end of High Street. There was also a small Wesleyan chapel beside Quill Hall Cottage opposite the end of New Road. This was replaced by another one near Blackhorse Bridge in Woodside Road. After the last war that was sold for redevelopment and the present St John's Methodist Church and hall erected adjoining the Fire Station towards the Sycamore Corner end of Woodside Road.

The Free Church, which started in a room at Turret House, the Avenue, acquired a site in Sycamore Road where they erected their first church in 1913 and later rebuilt it. Subsequently they took the opportunity to buy the commanding site on the Woodside Road-Sycamore Road corner where their postwar church and halls now stand. Both the Anglicans and the Free Church were well able to finance their present buildings from the great enhancement in value of the sites they had purchased which, except for the forecourt frontage retained by St Michael's, were sold off for the erection of shops and flats.

The Baptist Church, reached from High Street by a footpath beneath the archway at the side of the 'King's Arms', was built in 1784, although a General Baptist ministry is recorded as started in the town as early as 1626 by Richard Morris, who was stationed in Amersham when serving in the Oxford Blues. The books of the General Baptist community have their entries dated by the numbers of the months in Quaker style. Also showing further affinity between these early Baptists and the Quakers, there is evidence that they took each other in marriage after the manner of the Quakers.

This Georgian building is believed to be the only circular Nonconformist church of its period in the country. Within the square, mellowed brick shell this round church, with its old gated pews and spiral stairway to the gallery, rises to a central glazed dome. To the rear is the old graveyard, now mostly grassed over, with a fine boundary wall of 18th century brickwork along its west side.

The footway, paved with sandstone setts, continues from High Street through here and by a gateway into The Platt. Adjoining this ancient lane stands Chapel House, a slightly later Georgian building which was the church of the Particular, or Peculiar Baptists, an offshoot from the main body which soon died out. Partly burned down while unoccupied and later restored and used as a studio by a well known artist, this has since been converted into a private residence.

In a Parliamentary survey of livings dated 1649 it was stated that in Coleshill, a hamlet of some 200 persons, 'a church were fit to be erected and endowed with the tithes thereof amounting to £70, the people earnestly desiring the same'. It may have occupied the same site as the present small 19th century church, but traditionally it stood near Chapel Farm; although another location mentioned was Brainford (Brentford) Wood where some paving 'in a manner of dicework' was uncovered. Wherever it may have been, it was stated in 1832 when Coleshill parish was transferred from Herts to Bucks, that this chapel had been demolished 'about forty years ago'. There is also a small Baptist place of worship in the centre of the village adjoining Chapel Cottage.

Traditionally independent in both thought and action, the people of Amersham were amongst the first to assert their non-conformity in religious matters, especially in the face of the luxurious way of life of the English Catholic Church. The greatest preacher against the Establishment was John Wycliffe, whose followers in the 14th century became known as Lollards, a term which was later applied to everyone who displayed active opposition to the Church.

But it was not until the reign of Henry IV in the early part of the 15th century that a Statute was enacted which carried the penalty of death for religious nonconformers, who could be ordered to be burnt at the stake as heretics by the authority of the Ecclesiastical Court. It has been said that the labour question, with so many workers being low paid and half starved and the Church's indifference to this situation, was really the grass roots of the Lollard movement, and that it also included a growing political element. But what first hand evidence exists regarding the local Lollards and those who became martyrs, suggests that there was little political motivation but a strongly independent religious conviction.

After what was called the Seven Years Famine, followed by the Black Death during 1348 and 1349, the whole country was in a state of devastation and receptive to the disciples of Wycliffe who preached religious reformation. They came to Amersham barefoot, clad in russet gowns with staffs in their hands. The people flocked to hear them when they preached in the churchyard or the street. Many who responded to their crusading call journeyed to London to take part in the procession and demonstration in St Giles' Field in 1414. As a result of this, three Amersham men—William Turnour, John Hazelwoode and William Yonge—were sentenced and burned; and Thomas Cheyne, lord of the manor of Chesham Bois, had his estates forfeit and was imprisoned in the Tower for his participation.

In 1462 John Baron, Robert Body, John Crane and Geoffrey Simeon, tenants of Edmund Brudenell of Raans, were declared heretics. In 1506 the Bishop of Lincoln started to hold inquisitions in this 'hot-bed' of Amersham. William Tylsworth was sentenced and burnt at the stake in 'Stanley Close'; his married daughter, Joan Clark, was forced to light the faggots. Thomas Chase was taken to the bishop's prison at Wooburn, kept there in chains and beaten and half starved, and then taken out, strangled on the roadside and there buried as was the custom with suicides; it was announced that he had taken his own life.

Thomas Mann, a most ardent Lollard, came to live in Amersham where he won over many more supporters to the cause until he was apprehended and burnt at Smithfield in 1518. The Bishop of Lincoln held an inquisition at Amersham in 1521 which lasted for some months; many adherents were tried and imprisoned; Thomas Bernard, Robert Rave, James Morden, Thomas Holmes, John Scrivener and Joan Norman were condemned to be burned at the stake although the woman's sentence was reduced to imprisonment. Bishop Longland himself attended these burnings on the hillside above the town where he preached a 'violent sermon'. After that the persecutions died down.

In 1553 John Knox, who had been dismissed from his post as a chaplain to Henry VIII, commenced a preaching tour of Bucks. On the death of the boy king, Edward VI, Lady Jane Grey had been proclaimed queen to maintain the Protestant succession; in spite of their nonconformist tradition, the people of Amersham favoured Mary Tudor. On Sunday, 16 July, John Knox arrived in Amersham on his way back to London and preached in the parish church to a crowded and largely hostile congregation. He vividly recalled the occasion when safe in France two years later: 'In Hammershame when uproure was for establyshing of Marye . . . that unhappe and wycked womane'. Troops were called in to quell the disturbances which occurred after the service.

By the following day Lady Jane Grey was in the Tower and Mary Tudor on the throne. As a staunch Roman Catholic, she soon revived the Statutes of Henry IV and Henry V against Lollards and all other heretics. Due perhaps to Amersham's militantly expressed support for Mary, no burnings of local people are recorded during that time.

The stone obelisk in the field off Station Road is the Martyrs' Memorial erected in 1931 by the Protestant Alliance through the generosity of Miss E. M. Rowcroft. It records that, a short distance away, at Stony Plat, seven Protestants, six men and one woman, were burned at the stake: 'They died for the principles of religious liberty; for the right to read and interpret the holy scriptures and to worship God according to their consciences as revealed through God's holy word. Their names shall live for ever'.

Amersham again asserted its strong independence in religious matters during the 17th century when it became a notable centre for Quakers or, as they became known, the Society of Friends. Founded by George Fox, they gained no favour from either the Protestants or the Roman Catholics, nor with other religious dissenters and nonconformists.

The earliest reference to local Quakers is in 1655, six years after the execution of Charles I, when the country was slowly recovering and readjusting itself after the Civil War. By 1659 this new sect had many adherents in and around Amersham. Quakers presented a petition to Parliament for the abolition of tithes, an ecclesiastical imposition which they considered to be particularly unjust. Although this was in the Commonwealth period, the Puritans who had fought for, and gained, their own freedom of speech and conduct, were certainly not willing to grant the same tolerance to this new independent sect. In fact, under Oliver Cromwell and later under Richard Cromwell, a number of local Quakers were imprisoned at Aylesbury on the technical charge of non-payment of tithes; others were fined for refusing to take the oath in a court of law; and if they declined to pay, as they usually did, they also were imprisoned.

Isaac Penington, Lieutenant of the Tower and a former Lord Mayor of London, retired and bought The Grange at Chalfont St Peter. Later he handed over this estate to his son, also named Isaac. He had married the widow Lady Mary Springett, whose daughter Gulielma, then aged sixteen, came to live there with them. To the disgust of the staunch old Puritan, his son and his new wife and step-daughter joined the local Quakers, and soon meetings of the Friends were held at The Grange. A young man named Thomas Ellwood, from Oxfordshire, became friendly with the Peningtons, and to further his classical education, Isaac arranged an introduction to an able tutor in London—the poet John Milton.

In 1662 the Act of Uniformity was passed, resulting in the evictions of hundreds of clergy from their livings. This was followed two years later by the first Conventicle Act which expressly included Quakers. They soon suffered fines and imprisonment, with the threat of transportation into slavery for repeated offences of participation in conventicles, or private religious meetings. Both Isaac Penington and Thomas Ellwood, who had now become a Quaker, were destined to undergo various terms of imprisonment for their faith.

In 1665 as the Great Plague spread through London in the July heat, Penington and other Friends gathered in Amersham to attend the burial of Edward Perrot, a much respected Quaker. His name occurs in the Commonwealth State Papers as having set up a 'seditious paper in Amersham market house'. He had given part of an orchard at the 'town's end' (Whielden Street) as a burial place for the Friends, and was now himself to be buried there. A barrister named Ambrose Bennett heard about this while refreshing himself at the 'Griffin' on his way from his home at Bulstrode Park to sit as a magistrate at Aylesbury. He waited for the funeral procession, and as it passed by he rushed out and struck one of the bearers with the flat of his sword. In the scuffle which ensued the coffin fell to the ground. He ordered the arrest of the bearers and the other mourners, and it is narrated that the coffin lay there until the evening when the authorities had it buried in an unconsecrated corner of the churchyard.

Meanwhile Thomas Ellwood, worried about his tutor in London, found a vacant cottage at Chalfont St Giles and arranged for him to stay there until the plague had abated. It was at Chalfont that John Milton, with Ellwood's assistance, completed the revision of 'Paradise Lost' and discussed with him what was later to be 'Paradise Regained'.

Once again both Penington and Ellwood were arrested and imprisoned. Left alone with her daughter, Mary Penington could no longer afford to live at The Grange. So they moved to 'Berrie House' (Bury Farm) at Amersham. Here a new adherent to the Quakers visited them. William Penn, son of an English admiral and later to become the proprietor of what is now the State of Pennsylvania, USA, soon came to court the attractive Gulielma. About this time Thomas Ellwood, released again from prison, married a Coleshill girl, Mary Ellis, and moved into a small farmhouse down Magpie Lane, called Ongar Hill.

Some two years later the Peningtons had to vacate their temporary home in Amersham, and a local Quaker suggested they consider a farmhouse called Woodside on Amersham Common, which an uncle wanted to sell. So Mary and a friend named Anne Bull 'climbed the steep hill and came through Hills Lane'; but her heart sank when she saw the ruinous state of the house, and she returned home disappointed. A few days later Thomas Ellwood took her up there again, having meanwhile arranged the sale of a property she owned at Waltham; she decided to use the proceeds to buy and rebuild Woodside. Even so, the work took four years and proved a greater financial undertaking than she had anticipated. It was not without its dramatic moments, for she records that, while she was watching the progress of the work, 'part of the house fell down from the new casting of it, and in the falling I was most remarkably preserved'. In 1672 Isaac Penington was released from Reading gaol and able to join his wife at Woodside. Although his health was greatly impaired by imprisonment, he spent the last few years of his life peacefully here on Amersham Common, where his home stood until 1969 on the present site of the Community Centre.

William Penn and Gulielma Springett had become engaged, and in the spring of 1672 they 'took each other in marriage' at King's Farm, Chorleywood, and went to live not far away at Basing House, Rickmansworth. It seemed a happy prelude to this occasion for all the Friends when the Declaration of Indulgence was proclaimed by Charles II, granting freedom of worship to nonconformists. But it was conditional on each group first obtaining a licence to worship. True to their independent religious principles, the Quakers would not comply, maintaining that the worship of God should not be subject to official permits. Later, however, the King requested from the Sheriffs of the Shires particulars of all Quakers who were serving terms of imprisonment, and released them under a general pardon. So finally ended the intermittent persecution since the 14th century of all religious nonconformists. Nowhere did they display their independence more strongly, even unto death, than in and around Amersham.

The Parish Church through different eyes: ABOVE: as John Buckler saw it
in 1830 (probably a copy of the original); BELOW: similarly in 1838
(Both County Museum); OPPOSITE ABOVE: the local Broadwater view
in later years; and BELOW: through today's camera lens.

 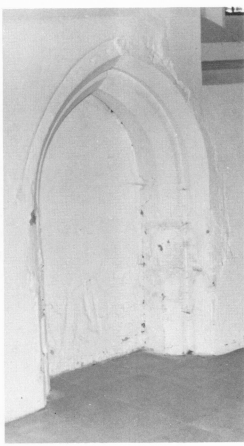

LEFT : The Broadwater record of St Mary's interior in the 19th century, and
RIGHT : the upper part of a doorway, in use before the floor was raised.

BELOW : John Buckler's drawing of the Rectory House
in 1838. (County Museum)

34

LEFT: Lollards were hanged and burnt at Smithfield in Henry IV's reign though local arrangements were less complicated than this.
(Mansell Collection)

RIGHT: This brass in St Mary's commemorates John Drake. The inscription reads: Sonne of Francis Drake of Essher, dyeing ye 2 of Aprill in the 4 yere of his age, 1623 lies here buried. Had hee liv'd to bee a man, this inch had grown but to a span . . .

BELOW LEFT: The Martyrs' Memorial off Station Road, and RIGHT: John Knox. (Mansell Collection)

LEFT: Isaac Penington and RIGHT: William Penn. (Both Mansell)

CENTRE: 'Barrel' and metal gravestones in St Mary's churchyard.

BELOW: The Friends' Meeting House in Whielden Street.

ABOVE: The Baptist Church up a yard off High Street.

BELOW: Amersham Choirs Festival, June 1934. (County Museum)

ABOVE LEFT : The Free Church in 1913, and RIGHT : St Michael's Church today, with BELOW LEFT : the Methodist Church in High Street, and RIGHT : St John's Methodist Church on the hill today.

BELOW : Bury Cottage (Windsor House) on the outskirts of Amersham Town.

Craftsman to Chemist

Within a predominantly agricultural economy, Amersham's lord let his lands not simply for rent, but encumbered with many conditions. Some relics of feudal practice were maintained by the Drakes even into the 17th century. Quarrendon Farm to the east of Coleshill was let at 6s 8d per acre. The farm ran to 300 acres of arable. Meadowland cost 10s an acre. If the tenant ploughed the meadowland, he paid an extra £2 an acre ploughed. Drake kept the timber, fishing, fowling, hawking and hunting rights. The fishing rights could not have been of much value on those hillsides. William Drake insisted on some acreage being put to orchards, and the hedges had to retain 'crab stock'—the lord had a tooth for an apple. On top of these and other requirements, the tenant had to give his lord two days' work with five horses and carts and two men every year, and two turkeys at Christmas. The tenant was expressly required to operate strict crop rotation.

Amersham's mills were also a significant part of the local economy for some centuries. A number of 17th century milling agreements have survived. The Lower Mill, Bury End (by 1825 a silk mill), was leased from William Drake by Robert Eeles by 1755 and was still in Eele's hands in 1778. Earlier, in 1665 Henry Goodspeed took a lease of Lord's Mill and died before the lease was up. His widow Elizabeth was 'lyable to Law which might force her to make good the covenants' for the mill's good order. She was released from her obligations.

In 1696 agreement was reached between William Mourton and William Charsley, and Mr Drake to build 'the New Mill' and to 'dig up the Old Mill'. As to the New Mill they were 'to make her fit to worck'. For this they would receive three stage payments of £10 and a final payment after the work was done of £30.

In 1766 another mill was constructed near Lower Mill, and lessee William Holding undertook to build 'one Good and Substantial Water Corn mill.' So the Misbourne was burdened with three mills within half a mile of one another—a different head of water must have been available in those days.

Direct evidence of the importance of timber to local crafts is reflected in timber agreements of the late seventeenth century, one of which concerned hoop-shaver John Bell of Coleshill, who in 1693 paid £243 for 54 acres of timber—except the prime trees. He had to cut and haul half his purchase between 25 March and 24 June, and the balance in 1695.

The Chilterns were always a forested district, largely of beech, so wood turning and carving were traditional occupations with local woodcraft principally applied to chair making. Although chiefly made around High Wycombe and Amersham, the chairs were called Windsors because they were taken to Windsor market to be sold to the dealers who came every week from London. They were taken from Amersham on packhorses along what is now a public footpath off London Road, between Bury Farm and a small period house named Bury Cottage (but which used to be called Windsor House because of this association), and down the valley beside the River Misbourne.

The chair parts were produced by 'bodgers'. These men lived throughout the summer months in the beechwoods, where they turned the legs, rails, spindles and stretchers on rigged-up and primitive but efficient lathes. Even in the 1930s, one of the last of these bodgers could still be seen at work just beyond the 'Queen's Head' at the turn-off to Winchmore Hill. Almost that late there was a chair works at 45 Whielden Street, where the long-tiled and timbered, open-fronted drying sheds backing on to The Platt are still preserved. There is a chair factory at Winchmore Hill but the manufacture there is with modern machinery. A small local cottage industry was the caning and rushing of chair seats which women and girls were trained to do in their own homes by the chair makers.

Agricultural wages were low until recent times, and various cottage crafts augmented the family income. Of these the best known were straw plaiting and lace making. The plait, which was made in various patterns (a local speciality being pearl or piping) was for the ladies' straw hat trade at Luton. Middlemen used to buy the wheat or barley straw from the farmers, prepare and bale it, and distribute it to the workers, at the same time collecting their finished plait. The average price paid was 1s 6d a score (20yd length) and the most one person could produce in a day, working from early morning till late at night, was about three of these lengths. To obtain slightly more money for their output, some women used to walk all the way to Luton and back—over 40 miles—to sell direct to the hat makers. Beyond the acquired skill, all that the worker needed was a straw splitter, and a tiny wooden mangle called a mill, for pressing the finished plait. In some places, such as Chesham, there were plait schools where children were taught the rudiments of education and learned how to plait at the same time. Even in 1871 there were still nearly one hundred plait workers in Amersham; but no record survives of a plait school.

During the 18th and 19th centuries pillow lace was another thriving cottage industry; and even in the 1960s one lace maker still worked at her craft in the Drake almshouses. Lace was introduced to Bucks and Beds by the Huguenot refugees from Flanders and France. In due course the various types of lace from Mechlin, Lille, Arras, Chantilly and other parts of the Continent evolved into the characteristic English pillow lace of which the finest was known as Bucks Point.

The designs were pricked on parchment which was set on the pillow (this was actually more like a small bolster) and marked out with pins. Then the white or cream thread was wound around the pins off bobbins. Made of box or any other close-grained wood, or sometimes of bone, the bobbins were often inscribed with names, texts, love messages or recordings of national events—a craft in itself. Except for the large bobbins used for the gimp to outline the pattern, and the very small ones used for Bucks Point, they had coloured beads, spangles or shells attached to the end by a loop of copper wire to weigh them down. Amersham became quite celebrated from the late 18th century for its lace of black silk (largely made up as veils) which was bought by the Paris dress designers for their latest creations. There was also a silk mill in Amersham. This stood in front of the present Scot-Bowyers factory and was pulled down in the early part of the present century to be replaced by the terrace of small houses which are Nos 35 to 41 London Road West.

In addition to the corn mills at each end of the town, one now a restaurant and the other a private residence, there was a flour mill on the site of No 55 High Street, now Lloyds Bank; also a woolstapler's in Keen's Yard beyond No 99 High Street where wool from the district was assessed for quality and value. Where the gasworks stands in The Broadway there was a tannery. Although there were cloth mills in Chesham and Chesham Bois, there is no evidence of any in Amersham. Yet as early as the 13th century a trader named German, of Amersham, is recorded as 'selling cloth contrary to the Assize', and a number of entries in the parish register give the description of cloth weaver. Also, one of the fields stretching up from the town towards Rectory Wood is shown on a tithe map as Tenter Field. In such places the tenter posts and hooks were fixed for stretching newly woven lengths of cloth; hence the phrase 'to be on tenterhooks'.

Brick making was another local industry. From the late 16th century bricks, tiles, pipes, pots and other clay products were manufactured around Amersham, including Winchmore Hill where the 'Potters' Arms' still commemorates this connection. Many of the old peg-tiled roofs in the town and the old bricks seen in the walls of the houses were of local manufacture. Attractive diapering has been formed in some walls by incorporating metallic blue vitreous bricks which, it is said, were produced by using furze, or gorse, to fire the kilns.

Although the Chilterns are basically chalk hills, there are considerable deposits of clay-with-flints. Whilst the clay was dug for brick earth, the flints were knapped and used with bricks to give variety to facing walls. The clay deposits to the north of the town had a lower oil content than those to the south. So brick making was mostly carried on along Copperkins Lane and in Chesham Bois (where the deep hollows beside North Road show where the clay was dug out of the common for the kiln which was on the corner of what is now Long Park), whilst pots and other coarse earthenware were produced at Coleshill and Winchmore Hill. Even in the 1930s, a forge stood at the roadside in front of the 'Fleur-de-lys' where the train of donkeys, returning after carrying their pannier loads of pots down to Amersham, waited to be re-shod.

According to Dutton Allen & Co's directory for 1863 there were then 46 crafts and trades represented in Amersham. By 1907 they had increased to 60 as recorded in Kelly's directory of that year. They included in 1863 all the usual country town occupations: corn millers, woollen and fancy drapers, greengrocers, boot and shoe makers, blacksmiths, carpenters and cabinet makers, carriers, ironmongers, painters, a watchmaker, tailors, a printer, bakers, undertakers, a dentist, wheelwrights, butter and egg dealers, butchers, hairdressers, builders, a wool stapler, chemist, schoolmaster, lace makers and straw plaiters; also six beer retailers in addition to the six licensed inns and the three hotels. By 1907 there were also newsagents, a dressmaker, stationer, coach builders, a seedsman, coal merchants, brick makers and lime merchants, an optician, fishmongers, plumbers and a milliner.

Of interest at the earlier dating were a letter carrier, a furniture broker, brazier, basket maker (in Station Road), stamp distributor, toy dealer, and a man who held a licence to 'let horses'. By 1907 the beer retailers had increased to 10 and there was a town cryer, an artist (Bert Jay on the Common), a person letting apartments and a provider of refreshments; the last two perhaps being aware, even nearly three-quarters of a century ago, of the potential of this historic and picturesque town as a tourist attraction.

There were 13 listed farmers in 1863 and 15 in 1907. The veterinary surgeon in 1863 was also a shoesmith, and in 1907 another veterinary surgeon doubled up as the Amersham sanitary inspector. Physicians and surgeons were consistent at three throughout the whole period, as were solicitors of which there were two. In 1907 there were also in the town two insurance agents and an accountant, whilst in addition to the auctioneer recorded before the middle of the 19th century, there was a firm of architects and house agents in Station Parade at Amersham-on-the-Hill.

By this time, too, an agricultural implement maker, who also owned and contracted steam rollers, had become established in Bell Lane at Amersham Common. This firm now has an international reputation for its sophisticated winches and other modern mechanical equipment. A volunteer fire service had been started (Capt G. Darlington and twelve men) with its 'fire cart' and primitive equipment at the old tan yard in The Broadway and the fire alarm bell under the market hall. The horses were those used during working hours for the coal carts. It is said that at the sound of the alarm, their drivers released them wherever they were and they would trot off to be harnessed up in the tan yard! It was not until 1928 that Amersham was the proud possessor of a motor fire engine.

The five general shop keepers in the town in 1863 had increased to eleven by 1907. There were also two cycle makers, one of which, with the advent of the motoring age, undertook the maintenance and repair of such few cars as were then on the road. During this first decade of the 20th century a sub-branch of the Union of London and Smith's Bank had been opened, and a branch of the Capital and Counties Bank, both in High Street. The Inland Revenue office had been moved from the 'Crown' to No 111 High Street where the rather short-lived Amersham and District Permanent Building Society was established. By 1907 however both the Savings Bank (a branch from High Wycombe) and the Literary Institute and Reading Rooms had closed down.

At Amersham-on-the-Hill (then Newtown) there was the Temperance Hotel and a sub-office of the main Post Office which was in the confectionery shop of Mrs Neville. In Station Parade stood the Bijou Hall. Owned and operated by the local firm of architects, it was advertised for entertainments and dancing with a capacity for 150 persons. It later became the Playbox cinema and then the Amersham Repertory Theatre and is now used as auction rooms.

The first shop below the railway bridge in Station Parade was a ladies' outfitters run by the Misses Peck; next door stood the Domestic Stores (owned by Mr Sumner who also appeared to practise as an architect); and the third shop was Chambers' grocery store. This was sold to the International Stores which later moved to the Chesham Road side of Oakfield Corner and subsequently around it into Sycamore Road where it expanded into a small supermarket, but has since been closed down.

The much publicised slogan of Mr Sumner's Domestic Stores was 'A store at your door with everything for the home at London store prices'. As a result of increased trade, this business was extended to what later became the 'Playbox', and further extended to the ground floor of Turret House on the corner of The Avenue. A little further down Station Road was a small general shop which is still there.

Theophilus Toovey, a furniture broker, originally had a shop adjoining the former 'Wheatsheaf' inn which stood nearly opposite Bury Farm in Old Amersham. Then he moved to newly built premises just below the railway bridge backing on to Rectory Wood, which he subsequently sold to J. Mead. The new owner started up a general outfitters' business which he later disposed of to Mr H. J. W. Renshaw whose sons still carry on the business. T. Toovey is said to have built Romney Cottage in Sycamore Road where he retired and died. It was later occupied by a well known theatrical family, the Thurlow-Finns. A shop with flats above in Chesham Road retains the name of this house.

Next to Nazing Cottage (built 1899) which backs on to Rectory Wood lower down Station Road, were Trowers', cornchandlers, who also had a retail shop near the Water-works in London Road. When this was taken over by the manager, Mr A. W. Pope, he transferred the Old Amersham business to Hill Avenue.

The Post Office and Telephonic Express Delivery Office in High Street received its letters from London and the south of England by mail cart from Slough at 5.37 am precisely; but from the north of England, Scotland and Ireland, letters arrived even earlier at 5.10 am after being collected off the mail train at Berkhamsted. All had been delivered by 7.30 am—and this was on seven days each week! Latest posting time for the first delivery next morning in London and the south was 7.50 pm. The letter carrier was not allowed to deliver a letter to any person in the street. In addition to the sub-office in Station Road, there was another in White Lion Road, also one in a cottage at Chesham Bois. Roadside, or wall, letter boxes were provided at Newtown, Hyrons Farm, Market Square, Bury End, Shardeloes, Woodrow, Coleshill and Winchmore Hill.

The main Amersham Post Office was open from 8 am to 8 pm on Mondays to Saturdays, and from 9 am to 10 am on Sundays for the sale of stamps only. Its delivery area (on foot or by heavy bicycle) extended to Little Missenden, Penn Street, Coleshill, Hyde Heath and as far as Sheephouses at the top of the hill beyond the present station at Little Chalfont. The neighbouring Post Office at Chesham also had a wide delivery area; but Amersham consistently retained its position as the main GPO Crown Office; for every time Chesham demanded a 'count' the Amersham volume of business proved to be the greater of the two.

By the early 1840s, a Chesham firm which ran a four-horse coach to and from Watford daily to connect with express trains in and out of Euston, also ran a coach from Wendover to London through Amersham, daily except Sundays, departing at 8 am and returning at six in the afternoon 'punctually'.

Benjamin Sills had a waggon leaving the 'George' in Chesham every Thursday morning at 11 o'clock for the conveyance of calves, sheep and lambs. It called at the 'Crown' Amersham at noon and continued via Chalfont St Giles, Maple Cross, West Hyde, Denham and Uxbridge, arriving at Smithfield Market at 3 am on Friday morning.

Other carriers of passengers and goods were:—
Robert Oldfield, Chesham to High Wycombe via Amersham, Friday mornings at half-past five and Saturday mornings at 10 o'clock; Joseph Holt from Amersham to Berkhamstead on Wednesdays and return the same evening, and on Thursdays from Amersham to Beaconsfield and Windsor; William Dormer to Berkhamstead on Tuesdays and Saturdays and between Chesham and Amersham on Thursdays; also Josiah Hall from Chesham to Aylesbury via Amersham, returning the same evening 'at a quarter before eight'.

By 1907 Edward Hillsden of High Street was undertaking a regular carrier service on Mondays and Thursdays through the Chalfonts and Uxbridge to the 'Lamb' in Old Bailey and on to 5 Bartholomew Close in the City of London, returning on Wednesdays and Saturdays. Also a service to High Wycombe was provided by Fred Free of Whielden Street on Tuesdays and Fridays. This was a day-return service leaving Amersham by 9 am 'promptly'. For the convenience of residents and other travellers to and from London by rail, an omnibus left the 'Griffin' each day to meet 'certain trains'.

The Amersham Bus Company was started at the 'Griffin', site of the first petrol pump (Pratt's Golden) in Amersham. The buses used to come into the inn yard around 28 Whielden Street and through the Crown Farm rickyard. The routes were Uxbridge to Aylesbury and Chesham to High Wycombe, going only to the top of the steep hill by the Royal Grammar School. The company also owned a char-a-banc called the 'Pride of Bucks'.

In 1830 George Stephenson planned a railway along the Misbourne valley through Amersham and on to Worcester. But although there was a petition signed by over a hundred residents to Thomas Drake, the principal landowner, so that the application could be made to Parliament, he refused to support it and the project had to be dropped. In 1846, at the annual meeting of the Buckinghamshire Railway, the directors reported that the line from Oxford to Bletchley and the line from Banbury to Tring would go ahead, but the line from

Aylesbury to Harrow (passing between Amersham and Chesham) would *not* be constructed. How different the subsequent development would have been if the Stephenson project had materialised, with a large modern town around the old one instead of a completely new town up on the common.

The Great Western Railway offered various facilities for Amersham residents who wished to travel to the West Country. One well known family named Cheese lived at Elmodesham House, High Street, from the latter part of the 19th century. They had a coach placed at their disposal at High Wycombe for their annual holiday. The whole family and staff, with heavy trunks and other belongings, together with ample food and drink, were transported there by horse-drawn vehicles and loaded into the coach. The next day this joined the train from Paddington for the long, and no doubt as far as the children were concerned, exciting journey to their month's summer holiday.

Amersham used to be a brewing centre, although not such a noted one as Chesham. Starting in High Wycombe, the Wellers came to Amersham about the middle of the 18th century when they took over all the buildings on the right-hand side of Church Street, now known as Badminton House and Badminton Court. Up the still cobbled yard opposite were their stablings and storage, and the buildings called The Maltings in Barn Meadow retain this name from the purpose for which they were built and used. Becoming the largest employers of labour in the town, the brewery prospered. The Wellers not only bought up increasing numbers of licensed premises locally, and in various parts of Bucks, Herts and Middlesex, but also acquired farms, land and property in and around Amersham. Through four generations this family dispensed their Weller's 'Entire' and grew wealthy on the proceeds. Then in 1929 the undertaking was sold at auction. The buyers, who were Benskins, were able to take over no less than 142 licensed houses, the extensive brewery buildings and various cottages and other local property.

After a rather chequered existence for nearly twenty years, Badminton Court was purchased soon after the last war by Douglas Collins. Completely modernised and considerably enlarged whilst still retaining its original character, this became the centre of an entirely new kind of industrial undertaking for Amersham, with the production of perfumes, powders, lipsticks and other toiletries under the much publicised brand name of Goya.

The chemist shop in Market Square was owned in the early part of the 19th century by a man named Broadwater. Starting a broadsheet mainly to advertise his goods, he developed this with local news and gossip, and in 1840 he registered it as a newspaper under the title of 'Broadwater's Journal'. It was published by the Agmondesham Press which was himself; he wrote and printed it in a room up the yard behind his shop.

Broadwater is reputed to have been quite a character, and one who said and printed what he thought, arguably one way to launch a successful local newspaper. He sold his chemist's business to T. H. King, whose family retained it until after the last war, and took himself and his newspaper to Uxbridge, renaming it the 'Buckinghamshire Advertiser'. There it was published on Tuesdays and Saturdays at 1½d a copy, with a growing circulation in the villages around, and in the western suburbs of London.

In 1880 a rival newspaper was started, called the 'Uxbridge Gazette'. Subsequently W. J. Hutchings acquired the Broadwater publication and after the printing works of the rival paper had been destroyed by fire about 1916, the two were amalgamated as the 'Middlesex Advertiser and County Gazette'. The present 'Amersham and Chesham Advertiser', with offices at Amersham and Chalfont St Peter, is one of its current series of weekly local newspapers.

The late George Ward, whose many photographs of Amersham and its people and events have provided such a valuable record of the town in Edwardian days, started as a printer with Ebenezer King, son of the Market Square chemist.

Amersham's other newspaper was founded in Chesham in 1892 as The Chesham Advertiser, ½d a copy. Now the Bucks Examiner, it maintains offices in both towns, and its independence as a single edition local paper.

Since the war light industry has developed rapidly, with the improvement of road and rail links with the metropolis, principally in the area between Amersham and Little Chalfont. Many nationally known companies have found their homes within the community. Perhaps the most outstanding example is the Radiochemical Centre of the United Kingdom Atomic Energy Authority, where the production of radio-active isotopes takes Amersham into the lives of the international community. Scot-Bowyer continue the Brazil tradition with their major processing complex for meat products, and the long established T. T. Boughton company engineers sophisticated machinery that finds worldwide markets. Music and book publishing, printing and packaging, aluminium and air conditioning, optics and plastics, prints and wallpaper, ties and tapes are among the many and often innovative outputs of an increasingly successful local industrial achievement.

ABOVE: Ploughing at Oakfield Corner c1900. (Mrs F. Payne)

BELOW: Amersham photographer George Ward's camera caught the haymakers off duty in this early study. (Ron White)

45

Bucks to wit A Register & Calendar of the Names and places of Abode of the Several Innkeepers Alehousekeepers and Victuallers within the Hundred of Burnham in the said County Licenced at the General Meeting of his Majesty Justices of the Peace Acting in the said Hundred in the Month of September 1753 As Appears by the several Recognizances returned into the Office of the Clerk of the Peace for the said County of Bucks

N.B. No Signs are mentioned in the Recognizances

Amersham

William Bodinson
Francis Dawson
William Deanchfield
Edward Pearce
Esther Parrott
Edward Deanchfield
Daniel Boddy
William Moreton
John Foster
Gersham Parson
Charles Fowler
Thomas Parker
John Child
James Wilson
Thomas Ghost
Thomas Penny

Burnham

Wm. ffield
Charles Cox
William Galley
Richard Stopp

LEFT: Amersham's licensed innkeepers, alehouse keepers and victuallers in 1753. (County Record Office)

RIGHT: Two trade tokens issued in the small change famine of the 17th century by Andrew Burrowes (1665) and Elizabeth Rutt (1668), and another token of 1797. (County Museum)

BELOW: Bury Mill before conversion into The Millstream. (County Museum)

ABOVE: The drying sheds at Amersham's last chair factory still survive—
at 45 Whielden Street (Lady Swiney), and RIGHT: typical Amersham
bodgers' finished products; ABOVE: the real Windsor chair of *c*1900,
CENTRE: a commodious variation of that period, and BELOW: the 1939
wheelback which has taken the Windsor name. (Eric Hearne)

BELOW: Sibley's Mill at the West end of High Street,
as it once was. (Staniland Pugh)

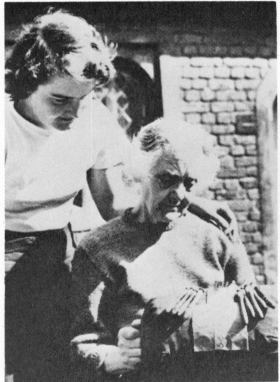

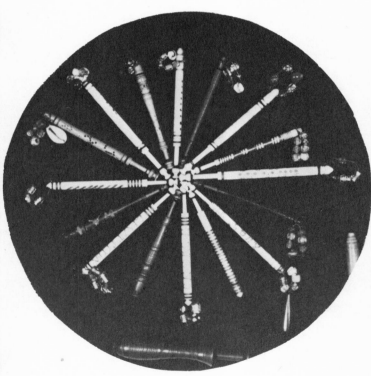

ABOVE LEFT: An Amersham strawplaiter at work at her mill, and BELOW: the last professional lacemaker in the town at her pillow (Bucks Advertiser), with ABOVE RIGHT: the Amersham black Bucks Point lace product (Arnold Baines), and BELOW: a display of local lace bobbins. (Isabel Pike)

ABOVE LEFT: Mr Beeson at work in Line's wheelwright's yard in the Broadway in 1860 (J. Hearn), and BELOW: horse drawn drays from Weller's Brewery (Ron White) with RIGHT: the famous local product.

ABOVE: Rock & Co of London published this print of the
church, town and brewery on 10 May, 1856
and BELOW: In 1891 Weller's 'Entire' is delivered safely to The Black
Horse, which gave its name to the bridge; (the embankment to the left
shows the railway under construction). (J. Hearn)

ABOVE: The first traction-engined dray at the brewery (T. Boughton), and
LEFT: The Brewery, now Goya's with, RIGHT:
the Maltings behind High Street.

51

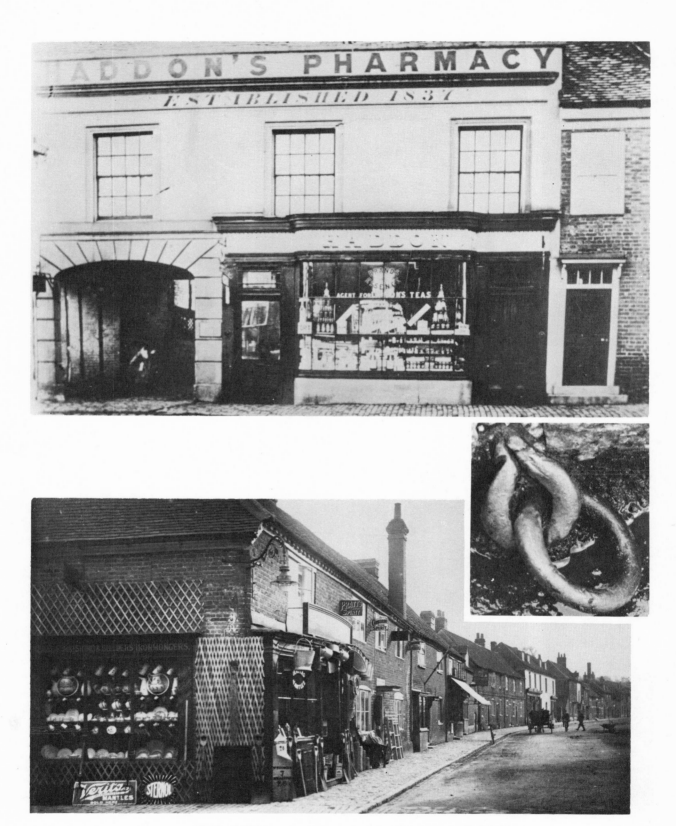

ABOVE: Haddon's Pharmacy at the end of the 19th century (L. Haddon), and BELOW: Whielden Corner in George Ward's day (Ron White), with INSET: the butcher's rings for tethering animals before slaughter, still in the High Street kerbside outside 39 High Street.

ABOVE: The Whiteside delivery van (they were located in Church Row),
and BELOW: the first Model T Ford van in Amersham
outside Hill's Stores. (Both L. Haddon)

LEFT: The '1372' sundial over E. Welch's Whielden Street shop in March 1934 (County Museum), and RIGHT: a Model T car from Flack's of Amersham a month later (H. W. Flack), with BELOW: Foster's Garage of Chesham Road—a more recent departure from local commerce.

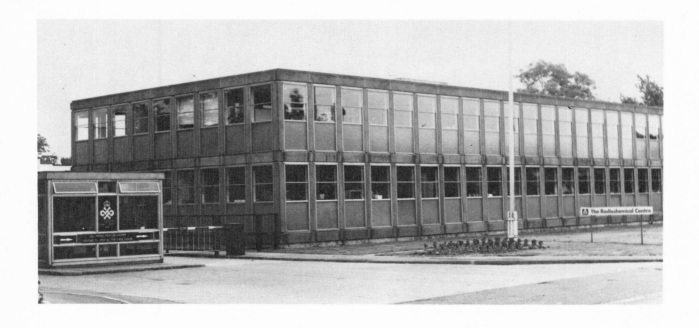

ABOVE: Amersham's modern industry with Scot Bowyer's London Road factory, and BELOW: The Radiochemical Centre in White Lion Road.

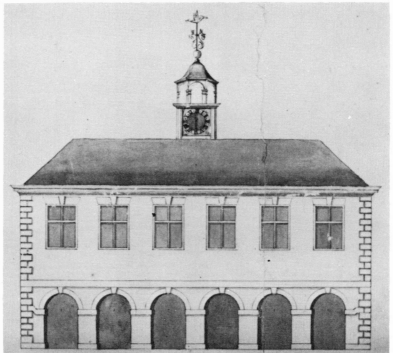

ABOVE: The Royal seal of Henry VIII on the original letters patent of 1508 exemplifying recovery of land at Amersham, Chenies, Chesham Bois and Chesham. BELOW: The original design for the Market Hall. (County Record Office)

Rights and Wrongs

The origin of Amersham borough cannot be precisely dated, but the 1200 royal grant of a market and fair may have led to the granting of some small burgage rights. In 1276 the 'fridboru' was held within a liberty thought to date to King John. By 1262 there is evidence of the town outside the borough. The borough court is included in the extent of the manor in 1299.

The borough organisation is poorly documented. Thomas le Provost and Robert and William le Budel or Beadle, together with John Portreve are recorded in the 13th, 14th and 15th centuries—names which reflect burghal offices. The 15th century local Fraternity of St Katherine was valued at the Dissolution of the chantries at £4 7s 6d.

The original charter granted a weekly market at Amersham and an annual two-days' fair. By 1526 the Russells had acquired the manor and in 1613 the Earl of Bedford surrendered the Friday market rights against the grant by James I of a weekly market on Tuesdays and an additional annual fair on Whit Monday. These rights were sold by the Russell family to the Drakes in 1637.

In the 17th century the people of the town considered forging a charter of Henry IV, but Judge Jeffreys smelt a rat and arrested James Child for procuring an exemplification of the charter by Charles II, and it was denounced.

Variously recorded as Elmondesham, Hagmondesham, Hamersham, Hamershame, Aumondesham, Aymondesham, Augmodeshame, Amundesham, Agmondesham, Agmodesham and Elmodesham, Amersham became a borough by prescription. It returned two members to Parliament on five occasions during the reigns of Edward I and Edward II but after 1308 there was a cessation until the 17th century when, after the petition to James I, the borough privileges were restored. Two members were returned in 1624 and then continuously until the disfranchising of all pocket, or rotten, boroughs by the Reform Act of 1832. Also under this Act, the detached part of Hertfordshire called Coleshill was transferred to Buckinghamshire.

Amersham as a parliamentary seat disappeared not simply because it was a pocket borough, but also because it could not be extended into other seats to form a reformed constituency—it was too closely bound by Aylesbury, Wycombe, and Hertfordshire, due to the Coleshill Herts enclave within Bucks.

Amersham's members—one of whom was usually from the Drake family—included a number of quite well known men. Edmund Waller, the poet, who was born at Coleshill, was elected in 1627, 1630 and 1631, to be succeeded by his son, also named Edmund, in 1688, 1689 and 1695. Algernon Sidney, executed for his supposed part in the Rye House Plot, sat for Amersham in 1656. Charles Cheyne, lord of the manor of Chesham Bois, who represented Amersham in 1653 was created Viscount Newhaven in 1681. His son, the second and last viscount, was elected for both Amersham and the County in 1698 following the death of his father, and continued this representation until 1705. One of the members in 1747 was Sir Henry Marshall, who two years previously had been Lord Mayor of London. But from 1768 to 1831 Amersham was represented in both its seats by the Drakes and Tyrwhitt Drakes to the complete exclusion of every other candidate put forward. The actual borough of Amersham comprised only about half of the town—the half owned by the Drakes!

During the earlier periods many who stood and were elected to represent the borough had never even visited Amersham. There is the well known story of one Parliamentarian who was journeying away from London one night when his coach broke down. Getting out, he asked his driver where they were. The man replied that it was a town called Amersham. 'Goodness me', was the startled response, 'it must be the place I am MP for'.

But in the 18th century Amersham represented landed interests. There were 70 'scot and lot' voters, and Drake patronage extended from the 18th century to 1832. By 1760 the lord owned most of the houses in the borough itself—a position gradually built up since 1742.

Despite their patronage of and stranglehold on the town's voters, the Drakes were held in high esteem, for their 'gentlemanly conduct, great liberality and hospitality'—a rare tribute to representatives 'elected' by security of tenure. The Drakes spent heavily at election time; £350 was a sum quoted in the 18th century, and this had risen to £600 in the 1820s.

The Drakes believed sincerely in their right to represent their tenant/constituents. Said William Drake in the House in 1790: he was one of a chosen band who thought for themselves, who were neither spaniels of ministers, nor the followers of parties.

The market itself almost lapsed in the 1920s, but was partly revived when a local grazier and butcher, Mr Arthur Stevens, would tether a bullock or heifer in Market Square and toll the bell.

Efforts were made in 1973 to revive this charter grant as a modern weekly market, by a commercial organisation which was promoting such markets in other old towns with dormant rights. The lords of the manor, the Tyrwhitt Drakes, who still hold these rights, were prepared to agree. It was opposed by both the town and district councils, largely because of the obvious congestion it would cause with the now heavy traffic through the town. It was then provisionally agreed, after various alternative sites to the main street had been considered, that a modern stall market could be accommodated on the public car park off The Broadway, the use of the rights being granted to the Chiltern District Council. Later, as the Council seemed to be taking no definite action in the matter, the commercial organisation again made a direct approach to the Tyrwhitt Drakes to hold a weekly market in High Street; this apparently could be done without any application for planning permission for up to a maximum of fourteen occasions in any one year.

An 1838 copy of Buckler's view of the Market Hall. (County Museum)

1789 whit fare

			£	s	d
Toamas Stavens	Thomas Stavens			1	8
Jams harn	James Heare			5	2
Jonasf hour	James Hoare			5	6
Jaun Day	John Day			3	0
Jorg huarey	George Quarrey			3	6
fasay	Sapey			2	6
hofall	Hofeld			1	0
Canon	Ann Cannon			1	0
Bod Day	Benj Boddy			1	2
1 Stool				1	2
3 Crockney stalls				3	0
turn rounds				1	0
Sheep	at Buff heeps			7	11
pigs & Cows				2	4
Gangon hread Stool Gingerbread Stall				1	0
3 Stools				3	0
2 Stools				1	6
On Kins & Stools sundrey Hawkers &c			1	6
Jon Saltan not pad 2		£2	12	11
			2	0
Charbal Expences	0	10	6
		2	2	0
			1	2
	£2	4	7

The tolls and charges for the Fair in 1789. (County Record Office)

59

ABOVE: This unhappily faded 1742 map of Amersham has Squire Drake's properties marked and listed—they represented a majority; BELOW: Landlord Fowler of The Crown Inn receipts the squire's bill for election entertainment in 1795. (Both County Record Office), and INSET: Amersham's poet-politician Edmund Waller. (Lord Burnham)

ABOVE: The voters of Amersham expressed their appreciation to their
Drake Member of Parliament on 2 April, 1784 and BELOW: in 1840 this
is what the town looked like to the Tithe Commissioners.
(Both County Record Office)

ABOVE: The Fair in September 1936, and BELOW: the Market Hall today.

Due Care and Detention

In 1657 Sir William Drake, Bart, built a group of almshouses in the town. Set around three sides of a courtyard enclosed by a brick wall and entered through a square-headed archway, these are of characteristic Jacobean architecture in mellowed brickwork with tiled roofs and stone mullioned windows. As stated on the tablet opposite the entrance, they were 'for the relief of six poor widows well reputed in the Parish'. The trust provided that these were each to be given seven shillings per week and, in addition, 9s 4d on the longest day of the year and 1s 4d on the shortest day. Also they were to receive two loads of wood and coals annually, and be given a new gown every two years. This, the inscription asserts, the donor considered to be 'a very good allowance for ever at his own cost and charge'. The accommodation for each inmate consisted of a good-sized bed-sitting room, small kitchen and a large coal cellar.

Although the conditions of this charity were for long faithfully fulfilled, it was obvious in more recent years that the income from the 17th century trust funds could no longer keep pace with inflation. The accommodation had become old-fashioned. So in 1964 the trustees converted the coal cellars into bathrooms, and modernised the building overall. As the trust conditions could no longer be maintained, instead of receiving payments, the occupants gladly paid a small weekly rent.

In 1875 a local person, Miss Day, founded almshouses in Post Office Yard for eight elderly females, married or single, with the stipulation that they must be members of the Church of England. These almshouses, reached through a passage at the side of 57 High Street, are built in one long terrace at right-angles to the main street and extending to the bank of the Misbourne, each with its own garden plot in front. The accommodation comprised a living room, kitchen, two bedrooms and a small back yard with a WC. Here, too, the bequest provided for a seven shillings a week payment to each occupant. But when the Drake almshouses were modernised, the trustees decided upon a similar procedure for these. They were modernised and the back bedrooms converted into bathrooms. The old ladies here were also quite willing to pay a small weekly rent.

Since the last war the Brazil Trust has provided an attractive development for elderly persons in Old Amersham at Whielden Green, off Whielden Street, and a block of purpose-built small flats called Galleons near the top of Station Road.

Originally the Amersham Poor House was at the Church House in The Broadway; then it was transferred in 1424 to what is now the Willow Tree restaurant to make accommodation available for the Latin school as is evident from the town map of 1742. Later it was moved to what is now 22 to 28 Whielden Street. At the end of the corridor on the top floor there was a tiny room with a heavily timbered door with a metal grille. This was used to confine obstreperous inmates. The door, marked with the 'broad arrow' is now in No 28. When they became an increasing burden on local finance it was decided to 'set the poor on work'

—making wool into yarn. From 1729 there are entries in the parish accounts for the purchasing of wool: 'three packs costing £7 1s 0d'. Further entries show where the yarn was sold: 'Carriage of yarn to Uxbridge, Mr Turner £1 5s 0d'.

George Gilbert Scott, the well known Victorian architect, was a Bucks man. Born at Gawcott where his father was vicar, he later came to live with his uncle, the rector of Latimer, to be coached in mathematics. During his earlier professional period he carried out a great deal of Poor Law work which ended in 1838 with the completion of the Amersham Union. This impressive set of buildings in brick and flint with decorated gabled and tiled roofs in Tudor style, stands at the far end of Whielden Street which, for some years afterwards, had its name changed to Union Street. Accommodation was provided for between 300 and 350 inmates, the infirmary being added in 1906.

The Amersham Union area comprised Amersham, the Chalfonts, Chesham, Chesham Bois, Chenies, Coleshill, Penn, Seer Green, The Lee, Great Missenden and Beaconsfield, with a population in the mid 19th century of 18,212.

Maintained as a workhouse for over a century, the Amersham buildings were partly occupied at the outbreak of the last war as an evacuation hospital for St Mary's, Paddington, and a number of prefabricated huts were erected on spare land beyond. In due course the remainder of the workhouse was taken over and the whole complex is now the Amersham General Hospital. The two massive tower blocks since erected here (without planning approval as they were for a public board) raised even more outcry in what has now become a conservation area than had the two huge gasholders which disfigured The Broadway when erected some years earlier.

In addition to the charitable foundations of almshouses, there were a number of other local charities, most of which were so small that they have since lapsed. These were provided by the income from funds invested in property, stocks or land (such as the continuing Bent bequest to the parish church incumbent) and distributed either as money or bread to the 'deserving poor' of the town. They included those of John Cheyne (1578), Agnes and John Bennett (1604), William Child (1621), William Tothill (1627), Nathaniel Snell (1627), Andrew Hall (1695) who left a cottage for occupation by a poor family, Edmund Waller (1699) and the oddly named Eleemosynary by William Drake the Younger which was for the supply of kindling wood.

The Tothill and Snell charities are still carried on and are well in funds, largely because they were originally for the apprenticing of local boys and girls (costing about £5 to £8) which is no longer practised. So the income in recent times accumulated, and approval was obtained some years ago from the Charity Commissioners to dispense it as grants to students and other trainees for the purchase of uniforms, outfits, tools or other equipment, and for travelling expenses to their places of training.

Law and order lay for centuries within the courts baron of the lords of Amersham's manors, but by 1299 the borough court was operating within the manor. Constables were appointed to the court baron from the burgh up to the 1850s. Their existence helped to recover parliamentary representation in 1624, proving as it did the burghal rights and privileges. Parish constables were paid £1 15s for travel and other expenses in 1618, and the Michaelmas Quarter Session was held at Amersham by 1681.

Two years before that three Amersham revenue collectors were indicted for extortion—John Webbe, Thomas Greene and John Batchellor snr. Henry Paley was in trouble for keeping a disorderly alehouse.

Even the squire was not exempt from justice. In 1679 Sir William Drake, was presented by the Little Missenden constable for failing to maintain a footpath. Two years later Joseph Tallboys, 'a person of evill fame and behaviour', was ordered to be removed from the town, and in 1683 Sunday traders were in difficulties when Thomas Peirce and Andrew Borrow of Amersham were presented for selling goods on the Sabbath; William Tench was before the court too for 'trimming on the Lord's Day.'

In 1686 Timothy Wingfield was told to swear in as a petty constable or be indicted for contempt of court, and restrictive practices were upheld when Giles Child and Richard Webb were indicted for trading as bakers without serving their apprenticeships, though Webb was found not guilty the following year. Dudley Pennard's appeal against his rates was referred elsewhere. His appeal was deferred again the following year together with those of seventeen other residents, including Wingfield Webb and Dr Tanner. Their appeals were subsequently dismissed. The appellants complained again in 1690, and justices were appointed to hear their comments.

The justices reported to the court at the Chesham Sessions. They found the rates were 'very uncertain and not to be determined without a generall Survey of the said parish, which would occasion a very great Expence and trouble to undertake.' They appointed 'eight discreet and indifferent persons . . . by consent of the Partyes who were aggrieved', and after further disagreement two further 'indifferent persons', to deal with the remaining objections of Sir William Drake, James Ball and William Child, the last two of whom agreed an amended rate. The squire's complaints were to be settled through his agents.

That same year Robert Hopper of Amersham was granted a County pension of £2 a year for war service, 'to his late Majesty, King Charles the second'.

Two years later Christopher Abbitts, labourer, was indicted for practising as a barber-surgeon without serving his apprenticeship, and Elizabeth, wife of Jonathan Ball, and Mary Ball and Anne Ball, together with Sarah Robinson and Susan Webbe were sent to Aylesbury bridewell for a month for 'night walking' and being 'notoriously known to be persons of ill fame and disorderly conversations.'

The court subsequently heard that due to the negligence of Joseph Tench, Joseph and Nathaniel Chearsley, Thomas Wright and Edward Hatch, who were supposed to watch them, the women 'fledd from Justice'.

In 1693 Matthew Evans, gentleman was indicted for breaking into John Browne's house and stealing a gun worth 5s and 15s in 'numbered money'. He was bound over in the sum of £100, to appear again. Edward Learhead dismissed his apprentice Mary Gates, and refused to re-employ her. The court ordered him to pay back £3 10s of the £4 the parish provided when she was first bound to him, and he was fined 3s 4d.

Local administration suffered another setback in 1696 when inhabitants alleged three people had been irregularly appointed Overseers, one of them 'not of Ability to serve'. The appointments went ahead, but enquiries were organised. Two years later Jonas Harding, one time Overseer was told to hand over 'a parish book wherein Entryes are made of the Poore rates' which he had 'secreted and withheld . . . to the manifest wrong to the inhabitants.'

Worse trouble was afoot as the century turned, when Richard Mason was indicted for falsely accusing John Tanner of inciting him to murder Timothy Child. At the same court Daniel Anderson, lace buyer was in difficulties for concealing the poor rate records, and petty constables William Hobbs and Henry Norwood were accused of not ensuring the right measures were in use at Amersham market. Anderson was ordered to return the rate book or be committed for contempt of court. The constables protested when their problems were referred to the Judges of Assize, claiming 'onely the Lord or Owner of the Markett' should have been presented. Nonetheless, a year later the constables brought to court cases against Isaac Carter and Jonathan Reading for keeping unlicensed premises, Richard Tapping for selling beer to Carter, and Edward Collett for trading in corn and meal without a licence. Collett was released and the proceedings quashed.

In 1710 Robert Lane wrote to the Sheriff's Officer seeking action against John Wade, James Clark, Robert Buffinton, John Hill, John Winfeild, Paul Line and Timothy Winfeild, for not looking after their stretches of the Misbourne's banks, to the damage of Mr Wyrley's Mill.

Time passed, and the County Police were formed in 1857. Nine years later the County's second Chief Constable was an Amersham man—John Charles Tyrwhitt Drake. Of him Lord Chesham said 'He is well up to the standard required . . . I do not think we could find a better.'

Drake was not impressed by the way his new charges gave evidence. He arranged mock courts. He organised the first promotion exams. He worked hard and forged a reputation for fair dealing with his men. In 1889 he was paid £330 per annum. Of 13 police stations, the nearest to Amersham was at Chesham. Drake retired in 1896.

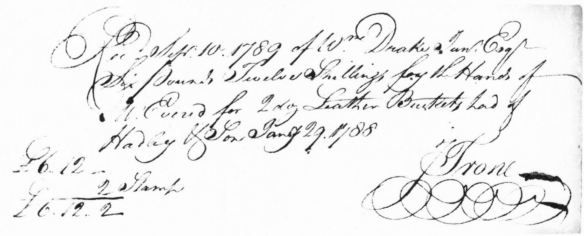

ABOVE: Drake's Almshouses, and BELOW: another Drake benefaction—
for buckets for the town's engine—in 1788. (County Record Office)

LEFT: Miss Day's Almshouses, behind High Street, and RIGHT: the solitary confinement cell door from the 18th century workhouse at BELOW: 22-28 Whielden Street. (Mrs Patteson)

LEFT: John Eaton reported on the workhouse on 14 August, 1746.

RIGHT: The 1754 record of the manorial court—
the view of frankpledge.

LEFT: A county police baton from Amersham; RIGHT: the old police station in High Street in 1932 (County Museum), and BELOW: the modern police and court complex in Chiltern Avenue.

ABOVE: The 1888 Amersham Union, now General Hospital,
and BELOW: the 1970's Health Centre.

On Parade

There is a local tradition that the Danes fought the Saxons at Gore Hill—the name certainly suggests bloody conflict, but the word first acquired its sanguinary association in 1563, and the old English 'gor' means filth. It may be the name derives from the state of the original track. At the same time, it is true that the Saxons faced the Danish invaders in The Vale of Aylesbury in 921 AD, and we also know the Danes, who first appeared off our coasts in 832 AD, moved up the Thames through Maidenhead towards Reading, which they reached overland. Did they strike north across the Burnham plateau as well, to attempt a link with the Icknield Way? There is no evidence for the tales of a Battle of Amersham, only conjecture.

Other early conflicts seem to have bypassed the town, and the levy of Ship Money by Charles I, which contributed so largely to the outbreak of the 17th century Civil War had no direct connection with Amersham, although John Hampden, who made the historic stand against this tax, lived only a few miles away, and the land for which he was assessed at 20 shillings was Honorend Farm at Prestwood. At his trial one of the judges, Sir George Croke, uncle of the rector of Amersham, gave his judgement in favour of John Hampden although he himself was a strong Royalist.

No actual fighting occurred near Amersham during this war of Parliament against the King, but the town was one of the key defence points for the City of London and the headquarters of the Buckinghamshire Lieutenants. Not only did Amersham people subscribe ardently to the petition demanding that the King's 'wicked councillors' be brought to justice, but they also contributed to Hampden's appeal for funds, and enthusiastically enlisted as his troopers.

From then on, Amersham was enlivened by the passing through of musters between Aylesbury and London, and received news of the subsequent engagements. After the battle of Aylesbury in 1642 Cromwell was given a great welcome as he marched through the town to Chalfont St Giles where he stayed at The Stone while his troops were encamped and resting there. Three years later it was at the 'Griffin' in Amersham that he stopped for refreshment when travelling to Uxbridge to meet the King's Commissioners. Following the decisive defeat of Charles II at Worcester in 1651, there is the following expenditure entry in the Amersham parochial records: 'Paid to Walter Webb and thomas todd for bread and cheese carrryed to Beconsfield to the prisoners taken at Wooster fight'.

By contrast, Amersham's Rector, Benjamin Robertshawe referred to the post-Protectorate town in 1731, mentioning 'Mrs Cromwell, Oliver's wife, and her daughters, at Woodrow high house, where afterwards lived Capt James Thomson; so the whole country was kept in awe, and became exceedingly zealous, and very fanatical, nor is the poison yet eradicated, but the Whartons are gone, and the Hampdens a-going.'

In 1912 Amersham was chosen as the location for the manoeuvres of the Regular Army.

They camped in Cowhouse Meadow (between the Shardeloes lake and the main road), up Gore Hill and at Bury Farm.

In the 1914-18 war, after Lord Kitchener had inspected the camp of the King's Royal Rifles (13th Battalion) at Halton and decided it was quite unfit for occupation, it was arranged for the men to be billeted in surrounding places, 'A' Company coming to Amersham. Mostly they were accommodated in the town, with the assistance of the Shardeloes steward who knew all the tenants well and how many rooms they could make available. But some had to go 'up the hill' and there is a house in Chesham Road which has still retained the chalk marks scrawled by the billeting officer on the wall beside its doorway, indicating how many men of 'Kitchener's 4th Army' were to be lodged there. They remained in training at Amersham until spring of the following year before proceeding to a west country transit camp and so to the front line in France.

Following Munich, a little over two decades later, preparations were begun for civil defence and for the evacuation of children from London into rural areas.

First-aid and rescue services were assembled. The local Red Cross and St John units organised first-aid classes and started cadet divisions for teenagers. Similarly the Council began instruction courses for the rescue and other services.

The report centre was in the Council's offices and the casualty personnel were accommodated in Keen's Yard, High Street, and in a vacant shop near Sycamore Corner. In addition, Dr H. J. Henderson formed a mobile medical and first-aid unit.

As Amersham was more than 25 miles west of London, some residents in the early days thought that all these arrangements were unnecessary. But, in fact, during the active period of the war over one thousand high explosive bombs were recorded in the Amersham district, as well as hundreds of incendiaries, and later flying bombs and rockets. However, casualties were caused in Amersham only at Stanley Hill and, unfortunately with deaths, in Chestnut Lane; but considerable structural damage resulted from bomb blast which, in this undulating chalk area, often occurred some distance from the impact sites of the bombs. In a number of instances such damage was not even noticed until years later they were revealed during routine survey inspections.

Not only did Amersham become one of the outer London defence points (as it had been in the 17th century civil war) manned by the Home Guard, but military training and transit camps were built in Rectory Wood and Pipers Wood where, even now, some of the foundation brickwork can be seen amidst the undergrowth. For the benefit of the reformed 51st Highland division, the Oxford & Bucks, Gloucesters & Middlesex regiments and others, a canteen was opened in High Street and staffed by the Women's Voluntary Services. Later Pipers Wood was taken over by the United States forces.

The final phase of the camp in Pipers Wood occurred from VE-day until after VJ-day when it served as a reception centre for returned prisoners-of-war.

During the war period, and for some time after, Amersham had its own British Restaurant at the Amersham Common hall in White Lion Road.

Much land was ploughed up, including Hervines Park and Shardeloes Park, for crop cultivation. Members of the Women's Land Army were drafted to work at Amersham, accommodated in the requisitioned former roadhouse and restaurant called The Cartwheel, in London Road near Cokes Lane corner. The local agricultural office was originally in such restricted quarters at the Amersham Union in Whielden Street that callers had to wait in the adjoining mortuary. Later an empty house was taken over up Westmount Avenue, off Station Road.

Amersham was on the route between London and Chequers, and throughout the war years cars would drive through, carrying British and Allied commanders, the Prime Minister and other members of the Cabinet, monarchs and representatives of governments-in-exile, premiers, ambassadors and other statesmen of overseas countries, and on more than one occasion, the King himself and other members of the Royal Family.

Although the majority of school children and expectant mothers were evacuated to greater distances from London, Amersham was notified to expect a certain number when the time came. Working from a house in Hervines Road, volunteers made a survey of every dwelling in Amersham, recording the number of occupiers and their willingness (or otherwise for various valid or indifferent reasons) to accommodate evacuees. In due course two complete schools arrived, one from Chiswick and the other from Clerkenwell. From the hall at St Michael's Church the labelled children were distributed by car loads throughout the households of the district. The vacated mansion of Shardeloes was taken over for expectant mothers, and during the war period many babies were born there.

Later, as a greater evacuation from London became necessary, mainly of those rendered homeless by bombing, mothers and their young children also found accommodation in Amersham.

As the war progressed, numbers from Amersham, as from so many other places, returned to London, but by the time the war had ended a number had become quite acclimatised and were so enjoying their new environment that they settled in Amersham, joined by their husbands; and their second and third generations are still here.

LEFT: Queen Elizabeth may have slept here, but Mrs Cromwell was a local resident (Mansell Collection), and RIGHT: John Hamden was a good and respected neighbour often in the town. (Margaret Sale)

73

ABOVE: An undated Ward photo of a military (and voluntary) parade in
High Street (Ron White), obviously a favourite rendezvous, as CENTRE:
in May 1934 The Bucks Red Cross (Amersham) ladies demonstrated
(County Museum), while BELOW: the Amersham Nursing Division of the
St John Ambulance Brigade gathered for this group portrait on
4 February, 1943.

Lessons Learnt

In earlier times education was largely undertaken and financed by the churches, in addition to which there were privately endowed schools and the so-called dame schools of questionable merit. It was not until 1870 that the State took a hand in the matter and schooling became compulsory.

Dr Robert Challoner, Rector of Amersham from 1578 until his death in 1624, was a cleric of some wealth although his forebears had been working weavers from Flanders who settled in north Bucks. He became a Canon of St George's, Windsor, and the Dean of Christ Church, Oxford. Just before his death he founded a free Latin grammar school in Amersham with three exhibitions to Corpus Christi College at Oxford University. The pupils were accommodated in the Church House which is now 1 to 7 Market Square; later they used the Market Hall.

In 1736 the master, Rev Benjamin Robertshawe moved into a house 'new built' in High Street which is believed to be No 111. In the wall of an upstairs front room there is a blocked-up doorway into No 113 which suggests that the master lived in one house and accommodated the pupils next door. After taking his BA at Oxford in 1702, Benjamin Robertshawe, son of a Lancashire schoolmaster, obtained the appointment to a 'vacancy in ye Free School at Amersham'. A year later he was ordained and then held curacies at Chalfont St Giles, Penn and Amersham where he became rector in 1728, continuing so until he died sixteen years later.

In an autobiographical manuscript he left he states: 'About ye year 1721 I was so unfortunate as to fall under ye displeasure of my Diocesan, Bishop Gibson (of Lincoln). The occasion was my refusing to bury a Presbyterian's child, sprinkled in their unauthorised way'. This child was apparently buried by the vicar of High Wycombe 'who, I suppose, would have given X'ian burial even to Pontius Pilate himself, provided he had but in his lifetime used to cry: King George for ever!'

A Latin school did not offer much local appeal as evidenced by the small number of scholars. Between 1800 and 1825 there were never more than four, and in 1819 none at all. But when the curate of Chesham Bois, the Rev Matthew Stalker was appointed master and brought his son with him to instruct in non-classical subjects, the number rose to fourteen. After his son died in 1830 it dropped to six. Even in 1895 when Kelly's Directory stated that the school had accommodation for forty boys, it added that the average attendance was only twenty-five.

In the massive ground floor timberwork of the school building in Market Square are the carved initials of scholars up to 1905, when a site at the top of Rectory Hill was acquired and new buildings erected and the principle of co-education adopted. After the last war, in spite of further extensions, this accommodation became overcrowded. So the girls were moved to the modern High School on the corner of Cokes Lane, Little Chalfont.

In 1699 Viscount Newhaven, the last of the notable Cheyne family of Chesham Bois, founded a Writing School in Amersham. This comprised a school house with an adjoining master's residence. These could also have been 111 and 113 High Street although the grammar school in Robertshawe's time was believed to have moved there. In any case, after the mid 19th century this school became amalgamated with Dr Challoner's foundation.

There were, at one time or another, various small schools in Amersham, and in the later 19th century the poor children at the Union in Whielden Street were also receiving regular schooling from a master and a mistress. A Miss Williams is known to have run a kindergarten in a room behind the chemist's shop in Market Square. Another person kept a subscription school, and two others together maintained a small boarding school; yet another school was conducted at Bridge House, Blackhorse Bridge, from which evolved the present St George's school in White Lion Road. Mrs Young kept a school in the Baptist Chapel which she later removed to Willowdene, High Street. The entrance doorway of the schoolroom at this chapel is headed 'British School'. This British School was established in 1842.

At Elmodesham House, High Street, now the offices of the Chiltern District Council, an academy was opened in 1829 by a Baptist minister, the Rev Ebenezer West for 'the education of the sons of Liberal gentlemen'. This establishment, which he had started in what afterwards became the Manse at Chenies, was so well patronised that it had to take over the small houses still to be seen up the pathway to the Baptist Church as additional boarding accommodation. The school gained a national reputation, for various of its scholars went on to have successful political careers, and three at least were appointed Privy Councillors. In 1860 it was removed to Caversham in Berkshire.

Although education had become compulsory in 1870, it was not until 1891 that Board schools were entirely free of the weekly pence (or two pence) system. At the annual Amersham Vestry in 1872 the rector, the Rev Edward Tyrwhitt Drake, offered to donate Wych Field in Back Lane as a site for a school to be maintained by the Church, assisted by voluntary subscribers. At the same time the lord of the manor donated a freehold property for a school at Woodrow. Financial support was given by the Diocesan Board of Education, and by the National Society which had been founded in 1811 to promote the education of the poor in the principles of the Established Church. In 1873 the original buildings of the present school were completed and opened by the Archdeacon of Buckingham. Additional land has since been acquired for the considerable enlargements carried out during the last two decades. This school is Aided but not Controlled; that is to say, although it receives State grants, it is still a Church School.

The Henry Allen Nursery School in Mitchell Walk provides a link between Amersham-on-the-Hill and the USA. It was established through the efforts of the late Senator Henry Allen of Kansas. Also in Mitchell Walk, Woodside was the first modern school built locally after the last war. It was visited and copied by various Continental education authorities.

Following a gift of land by the Viscount Curzon in 1847, and donations from the Tyrwhitt Drakes and other local families, Coleshill acquired a Church school in 1847. This comprised a schoolroom and master's dwellings, but in those days the attendance was poor. In 1858 'for every child present there were six absentees'. Small wonder, as the school hours were 8 am to 5 pm and, in any case, children were needed for all kinds of odd jobs in this rural community. Even in 1907 when the school had a capacity for 160 scholars, the average attendance was only 126. On each side of the entrance doorway are the marks where those who did attend sharpened their slate pencils when arriving.

In more recent times a number of small independent schools were established in Amersham. These included the Turret School, The Avenue, a preparatory school for both boys and girls; St Martha's in Cokes Lane, mainly for girls including boarders and conducted on P.N.E.U. principles; St Nicholas School, White Lion Road, which was a kindergarten and preparatory day school; Kingsley House School, Woodside Road, and the Becket School, also in Woodside Road, a Roman Catholic school for boys which still continues as a much larger educational establishment in rural surroundings between Orchard Leigh and Ashley Green. There was also the Amersham School of Music in Sycamore Road.

ABOVE: Amersham Grammar School in 1824—from a Buckler drawing
(County Museum), and BELOW: the staff and scholars somewhat later.
(Ron White)

LEFT: The title page of a notebook giving the accounts for Dr Challoner's Charity in 1623, showing the distribution of £10 10s to the town's poor, and RIGHT: the rents received in the Grammar School accounts of 24 April, 1691. (Both County Record Office)

Dr. Challoner's Grammar School,
AMERSHAM.

RULES.

1.—All pupils are required to wear the School Cap (in the case of girls, white straw hat in the summer and black felt hat in winter) with house ribbon and badge, on their way to and from School, and also when attending School matches, etc., Caps and badges may be obtained from the Headmaster (price:—Caps 2/3, badges 1/6, house ribbon (boys) 2d., house ribbon (girls) 2/-).

2.—The School Drill costume (a pattern of which may be obtained from the Senior Mistress) with a *plain white or cream blouse, is compulsory* in the case of girls for drill and hockey. It may also be worn at any time, *but only with the correct blouse and without underskirts.*

Girls must wear their hair plaited and tied with *black* ribbon only. No jewellery, except a plain brooch, may be worn in School.

3.—Boys must be provided with football shorts (blue), black and red striped football jersey, football boots, cricket boots or shoes, dark grey rubber-soled shoes for drill and indoor wear, and white shirts for cricket and drill.

Girls must be provided with a pair of slippers for indoor wear, and rubber-soled shoes for drill and tennis. It is advisable to keep an extra pair of stockings at School, in case of getting wet.

4.—Girls are not allowed to walk to and from School with boys, nor to travel with them in the train.

5.—Games and drill are compulsory, and no excuse except that of illness will be accepted. If a pupil wishes to be permanently excused, a doctor's certificate must be produced. In case of temporary indisposition, leave of absence from games and drill must be obtained *beforehand* from the Headmaster (or in case of girls from the Senior

ABOVE: The Rules in 1924 (Mrs C. M. Brown); BELOW: one of the school buildings on the Chesham Road site.

ABOVE: A classroom at Challoner's in 1924 (Mrs C. M. Brown), and
BELOW: a contemporary aspect of the Boys' School.

ABOVE LEFT: Elmodesham House, High Street, once Ebenezer West's Academy; RIGHT: 111/113 High Street—once the Master's House and Schoolhouse; CENTRE: British School 1842 plaque on the Baptist Church, and BELOW: Dr Challoner's Girls' School at Little Chalfont in 1976.

ABOVE: A pleasant if misty nineteenth century prospect looking up Church Street, in the Antiquarian Itinerary; drawn by W. T. Stockdale, engraved by E. Roberts (County Museum), and BELOW: that prospect is as pleasing today.

A Pleasant Prospect

The most easily obtainable and therefore traditional building materials for this part of the country were flints, and timber. Houses were timber-framed, usually of oak, cut and used to the natural growth shape of the trees so that the rest of the building had to be constructed to conform. The timbers were pegged, not nailed together.

Originally the wall panelling between the framing was a mixture of straw or furze with clay, called wattle-and-daub. Roofs were originally thatched, but hill corn produced such short straw that the thatch needed frequent renewal. With the introduction of brick making, the primitive walls, some of which had already been replaced by rough, unknapped flints, were built of brick, or else brick and split flints in patterning. At the same time peg tiles replaced the thatch.

Questions often asked are 'How old is this or that house?' or 'Which is the oldest house in the town?' Neither can be answered accurately, for all the really ancient houses have been partly or entirely rebuilt at later dates. Also, in the 18th century many of the half-timbered fronts were given a fashionable face-lift with an entirely new front of brick with Georgian windows and doorways. So to discover the oldest part of any period cottage or house, one needs to inspect the back.

Like most old towns, Amersham is laid out as a four-cross although in this case a staggered one, centred upon the church and the market place. The wealthy tradesmen and other influential people lived towards the west end of the town and the poorer people to the east, as was the traditional disposition in London, with its West and East Ends, and elsewhere. It is said that this was because the prevailing wind in this country has always been from the west.

Few similar small towns still preserve, as Amersham does, the general appearance of the 17th and 18th centuries. A noteworthy feature of High Street is its spaciousness, often stated to be the distinctive character of a coaching town; but much of the width of the present roadway from the Market Hall westwards derives from the late 19th century long front gardens of the houses along the north side of the street. The sidewalks were cobbled and pre-pedestrian crossings of cobbles were laid across the rough, unmetalled High Street roadway. Even so, Amersham was a coaching town, as evidenced by the numerous high-arched entries to what were the posting yards of the inns.

Formerly there were far more cottages at the town centre. The attractive Memorial Gardens occupy the site of a number of these, and there was a terrace running from beside the Willow Tree, in front of the gardens as far as the Malthouse, with a narrow passageway through to the churchyard. They had no gardens or even back yards to provide any privacy for the occupiers. Called Church Alley, they were demolished in 1939.

Occupying a prominent and central position between Market Square and High Street (and so fortunately slowing down somewhat the rush of through traffic) is the Market Hall, often incorrectly referred to as the town hall. Erected in 1682 by Sir William Drake (nephew of the baronet of the same name who founded the almshouses) and displaying the family arms, this is of red and blue brick and freestone with kingpost and tiled roof surmounted by a clock turret. The actual hall where the trade guilds held their meetings is supported upon arches above a paved area where local produce was sold under cover on market days. A notice displayed here states: 'Notice. In case of fire the sum of one shilling will be paid to any person ringing this bell. Caution. Anyone giving a false alarm will be prosecuted. By order. W. W. Drake, Esq. July 1892'. Built into the end of the market hall is the town lock-up, still with its heavy wooden door and rusted grille. Against the exterior wall is preserved the town pump dated 1785.

Amersham retains its fine old coaching inns, the most picturesque being the 'King's Arms' in the centre of High Street. Although this has been described as Brewers' Tudor, it was rebuilt from a small original inn and some adjacent cottages, and much of the timbering and other parts of the structure are genuinely of the 15th and 16th centuries. In the entrance lounge is an unglazed mediaeval window, and a massive Tudor staircase leads to the open-timbered Elizabethan upper hall.

The 'Griffin' in The Broadway has an impressive front of three storeys with attic dormers above. The interior displays heavy 17th century and earlier timberwork and what is claimed to be the remains of a chapel. This property came into the possession of Ralph de Wheilden after the dissolution of the monasteries. The original outbuildings, some now behind No 14, were used during the coaching era for overnight accommodation for drivers and postillions, with stablings for the changes of horses.

The exterior of the 'Crown' in Market Square belies its age, for it had to be refronted after a rather disastrous fire. It dates mainly from the early 17th century and retains a painted royal arms of Elizabeth I in the lounge. It still has half-timbered former stables across the cobbled yard called the Tudor Room. This hotel used to have a Georgian portico to its entrance, but this was damaged so often by passing traffic that it had to be taken down.

The 'Swan', at the west end of High Street, is of mellowed brickwork and exposed interior timbering. It displays the date 1671 which is about right. The 'Elephant and Castle' seems to be of a similar age but has been considerably renovated. The 'Chequers', in London Road, is of flint and brick with a renewed front. This was also built in the 17th century, as was the 'Saracen's Head' in Whielden Street. The 'Eagle', almost as old, is said to be one of the only two Bucks inns (the other being the 'Pink and Lily' at Lacey Green) which preserves that ancient game called Ringing the Bull. Two inns which have now disappeared were the 'Wheatsheaf' at Bury End, and the 'Old Griffin' in the tiny hamlet of Mop End which lies beyond Shardeloes upper park.

At 22 High Street where the rear buildings have now been converted into housing, the first service garage in the district was registered. The petrol pump, which stood up the yard until 1975, dispensing motor spirit at 6½d a gallon in the early days, was not installed until some years after the 'Pratt's Golden' pumps at the 'Griffin'.

Two of the oldest cottages in the town, dating at least from the 15th century, are the one on the left-hand corner of Church Street (15 Market Square) and 49 High Street. The latter, now unfortunately hidden behind a lock-up shop, was the meeting place for traders and townspeople before the market hall was provided. The smallest cottage in Amersham is 129 High Street; originally of two rooms only, its interior displays massive late 16th century timberwork. Although the 17th century terrace of cottages (165-189 High Street) in which no two are exactly alike, is called Turpin's Row, it has no connection with the notorious highwayman but was once owned by Thomas Turpin. Similarly the adjoining Fountain's Court does not provide any attractive water display but was owned by a local family of this name.

117 High Street, a bow-windowed late Georgian cottage, had a blue lamp over its doorway until about fifty years ago, for it was the town police station. No 119 next door is Georgian and earlier with a classic style doorcase. For long it was said that tragedies would occur to successive generations of the Drakes unless a member of the family lived in the dungeons. There certainly are deep underground cellars below Shardeloes mansion; but it was only when the title deeds of this High Street house were inspected not many years ago that its name was found to be The Dungeons!

The splendid Elmodesham House (42 High Street) was built by Charles Eels in Georgian days. Piers Place (a modern applied name with no historic or local significance) is a handsome Queen Anne residence at the west end of High Street although the annexe was added in the present century as a doctor's surgery. The plain brick Hinton House beyond it is Georgian, as is White House in Church Street; Apsley House (28 High Street), set back and with a medallioned double-bayed front, is of only slightly later dating.

In spite of its Georgian façade, the former 'Red Lion' (41 High Street) is some three hundred years old. It was noted for its vast inglenook and has what used to be an assembly room on the first floor extending over the rear courtyard on iron columns; there is also a powder room. The half-timbered and much restored Buckingham's Gate (No 39) used to be a butcher's shop, and the iron rings are still attached to the curbing of the pavement where the animals were tethered awaiting slaughter. No 57 adjoining Lloyds Bank is a three-storeyed, stuccoed Georgian building, now shops and flats, which was the Post Office before what is now the automatic telephone exchange was built in modern Georgian style at Amersham-on-the-Hill. Nos 105 and 107 are neat 18th century houses displaying good corbelling below the front eaves.

What must have been a fine Tudor residence, now divided into three smaller houses (56 to 60 High Street) is timber-framed on high flint and stone foundations, still retaining its characteristic 16th century chimney stacks. No 56 is of special interest for its contemporary wall paintings, dating from about 1550. They are on plaster panels around two walls of the sitting room where some of the framing timbers also retain traces of colouring. These paintings are of the Nine Worthies, top rating heroes in the Tudor chart. Although they cannot now all be individually identified, due to age and much past neglect when some were in a coal store behind a staircase and others in the back of a wall cupboard, they are known to be: Julius Caesar, Duke Joshua, King David, Hector of Troy, Charlemagne, Godfrey de Bouillon (who led the first Crusade), Alexander the Great, Judas Maccabaeus and King Arthur. Three are Christians, three Jews and three Pagans.

Other houses in Amersham also have remains of similar decorative wall work although many more must have been long ago destroyed or plastered over and lost. During redecoration work at 14 The Broadway in 1962 one complete wall of a front bedroom was found to be covered with Elizabethan paintings which have been dated as between 1580 and 1600. Downstairs in the same house further colour work has been found on some of the timbers.

Undoubtedly the finest and most interesting of all the period houses in Amersham is The Gables, 27 High Street. Brick built but rendered to give the appearance of stone, it has Dutch stepped gables and mullioned latticed windows. Allowed to fall into disrepair during and after the last war, it has since been most carefully restored. Except for a 19th century rear addition, it is entirely late Tudor. The two principal rooms at the front contain finely moulded fireplaces of Tottenhoe stone (known as clunch, being hard chalk) with heavily carved oaken overmantels added about 1640. Three rooms have late 16th century oak wall panelling with matching original doors and door furniture. Behind the front bedroom is a contemporary powder room with a small latticed window onto the staircase. The door of the smaller front bedroom is noteworthy as it is crudely adzed and obviously even older than the house.

Tresco House (33 High Street) is yet another interesting period residence with its 17th century half-timbered front now masked by a Georgian brick façade with contemporary windows and doorway. When the conversion of the extensive rear part of the property was undertaken, a brick vaulted bread oven was found which was so large that it is now half of a new sitting room.

38 High Street is an early 19th century building with ornamental ironwork above the shop front which dates from 1910. Until a few years ago this was Haddon's Pharmacy. In addition to the normal retailing of a chemist, it also originally sold tea, cigars, paint and Bibles, and held one of the rarely granted chemist's licenses for spirits in addition to wines. At that time, too, the owner was also an optician. Up the passageway beside the shop can be seen its tall brick warehouse, now converted into a private residence, with its massive pulley hoist preserved. This business was established in 1837 by an apothecary named Pike who soon disposed of it to Hailey Norton. He was succeeded by the chemist, Nathan Smith who used the warehouse for the manufacture of mineral waters (he had his own well fed by a spring of pure water in the shop cellar); he also produced agricultural fertilisers and his own speciality, dandelion coffee. About 1884 he sold out to A. P. Heald who, in 1892, disposed of the business to Albert H. Haddon in order to enter Medical School, where he qualified and then obtained a doctor's practice in London's east end. One of Mr Haddon's two sons carried on the business until a few years ago.

In addition to High Street, which terminates at Coldmoreham, a 17th century farm-house still retaining four large inglenook fireplaces, there are many fascinating houses and cottages along Whielden Street and up Church Street. Badminton House, in the latter and now converted into flats, dates from the 17th and 18th centuries and was once a coaching inn called Rumseys. It later became the offices for the brewery (Weller's 'Entire') at what is now called Badminton Court. 44 and 46 Whielden Street, 17th century but refronted, were originally one house. Here a quite vast bread oven was found (later converted into a children's playroom) and it is known that in the 19th century this was the communal bake-house for the town. 19 Whielden Street, with a sundial on its front wall, is certainly quite old, but the date on the sundial must be discounted.

There are attractive old half-timbered cottages along The Platt, off Whielden Street, and others in The Broadway where some original wattle-and-daub walling is preserved behind a sheet of glass at the Malthouse which had to be rebuilt after a fire in 1890. Broadway House (No 50), refaced in Georgian times, is basically Elizabethan, as confirmed by its title deed with a seal five inches in diameter. The half-timbered No 42 close by is distinctive for its front bedroom fireplace which is set with old Delft tiles. No 8 dates back to the time of William and Mary and retains an original bow window, as does No 28. The smithy in The Broadway closed down in 1958 and is only remembered by the name of the adjoining No 21, the 17th century Forge Cottage. It was transferred here from what is still called the Old Forge (26 High Street), now a well restored 16th century gabled building with an over-hanging upper storey. On a cottage (60 London Road) opposite the old bus depot (now a shop and service station) is a notice board dated 1811 which reads: 'The Magistrates acting for this Hundred have given peremptory orders to the Constables and other Peace Officers to Apprehend all common Beggars, Ballad Singers and other Vagrants so that they may be dealt with according to the Law'.

At the foot of Gore Hill stands Bury Farm, a historic house which was the principal building in the old hamlet of Bury End. It was purchased by Sir William Drake towards the end of the 17th century but the building is appreciably older than that. It has a close association with the early Quakers; for it was at 'Berrie House' that William Penn courted Gulielma Springett. 6 London Road West, adjoining the farmhouse, was where the Lollards held the Conventicle (meeting of dissenters) which is believed to be the first recorded in English religious history. About a mile down the Misbourne valley from the town stands a former mill, not old enough to be recorded in Domesday and, from its appearance, not even of mediaeval origin. Called Quarrendon Mill, this takes its name from the farm on the hillside above it, both deriving from the family of this name who were tenants of the Earls of Essex in the 13th century.

The Pest House, an isolated cottage which stood halfway up Gore Hill, was not much in use until the Great Plague of 1665 when people fled from London carrying the infection with them. Although those who reached Amersham were confined here, it did not stop the plague spreading, and the unfortunate townspeople who contracted it were put there with them, to live—or more likely to die—together. As early as 1625 the church accounts show a payment of £2 16s 11d for 'the releefe of such as were suspected dangerous to the parish in time of infection'; but it was not until 1688 that this isolated building was referred to as the Pest House. In 1740 there is an inventory of the contents 'Att Gore Hill House' including such items as: 'six chares, a pare of belos, one fire shovle, one warmen pan, a bead, five sheets, one bollster'. Subsequently this rather forbidding looking building with its black tarred exterior walls was converted into a private house, still retaining its name, until it had to be vacated and demolished when the old lane was replaced by the present 'A' class road in 1964.

Succeeding William Tothill, who died in 1626, the Drakes and the Tyrwhitt Drakes became lords of the manor of Shardeloes. Their impressive, classic style mansion was built in 1760 in replacement of the Tothills' old manor house which had acquired the usual distinction of Queen Elizabeth's overnight stay. It is doubtful if she slept well amongst the family of thirty-three children, if at all. This mansion where Queen Anne almost certainly did stay, and now converted into luxury flats, stands in an extensive and well wooded park beyond the west end of the town with a lake from which came the largest pike to be caught in England prior to the last war, when the lake was emptied for the silt to be used on the ploughed up parkland. Shardeloes was built by Stiff Leadbitter of Eton, although Robert Adam was commissioned to carry out the rich interior decorative work and is believed also to have recommended modifications to the general design, including possibly the inclusion of the handsome pedimented portico with its Corinthian columns. The construction is of brick, which was later stuccoed, and the family accounts show that 430,000 bricks were used for the house and as many more old stocks (largely no doubt from the demolished manor house the foundations of which can still be seen behind and to the left of the present mansion) for the stable block, orangery and other buildings. The total cost was £19,129 19s 4¾d. The name Shardeloes is from the Old English for a notched mound which could describe this location on a hillside ledge. In the park the old cattle fences were sunk in deep ditches so as not to spoil the views from the mansion.

Between the end of High Street and Coldmoreham stands Little Shardeloes, a dignified gabled residence now divided up, which was the dower house of the manor. At the rear is an attractive timbered building converted into a private house. The high flint and brick wall fronting the roadway bears the date 1688 and the initials "C.H." A cul-de-sac of modern Georgian style houses now occupies the former gardens.

Most of the houses and cottages in Old Amersham are listed Class II for preservation, and the town itself is now scheduled as a conservation area. Over a long period local efforts have unsuccessfully urged a by-pass. Traffic has become heavier, with increased danger alike to pedestrians (there have been many serious accidents and deaths) and to buildings. Whilst the timber-framed houses are able to move with the vibrations from the heavy passing vehicles, the Georgian and later brick buildings have developed dangerous fractures and settlements.

Earlier refusals for a by-pass were justified by suggesting the traffic flow did not warrant it, in view of the more pressing needs of other towns. But when such a reason could no longer be sustained, the refusals were based on insufficient finance. However, some years ago the project did reach the stage of a published plan offering various alternative schemes, all of which incorporated a link road from Chesham, which received no support from this neighbouring town.

The alternative Amersham by-pass routes suggested were on the north or the south sides of the town. The former would be from Mantles Green, behind School Lane, across Rectory Hill and Station Road to a roundabout just beyond Chequers Hill; but this did not meet with local approval, and as the County agreed, had many disadvantages. The southern route was over Shardeloes park, across Whielden Street just beyond the hospital on a viaduct, then over Gore Hill (which before this had been reclassified as an 'A' class road) to a terminal roundabout beyond the bottom of Stanley Hill, as on the other route. This scheme met with general approval. With increasing economies imposed on public funds, however, the whole proposal had to be shelved, and the Amersham by-pass now looks as far away as ever it was.

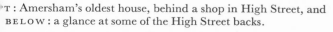

ʀᴛ : Amersham's oldest house, behind a shop in High Street, and
ʙᴇʟᴏᴡ : a glance at some of the High Street backs.

ᴠo vanished Tudor murals once next door to the old Grammar
School—the right hand one is Hercules.

ʜe Crown Inn when it boasted a fine portico, victim to road
ᴇ (Staniland Pugh), and a 19th century Crown billhead.

ABOVE: The Griffin, mid-19th century (County Museum), and BELOW: The King's Arms earlier this century, when oils and petrol vied with beer for custom.

ABOVE: The King's Arms in all its timbered glory—based on buildings
of the period and genuine timbers from elsewhere.

BELOW: Chimney Cottage, The Platt—a 17th century survivor.

91

ABOVE: The once Georgian chapel, now Chapel House, The Platt; RIGHT: detail from the magnificent Tudor overmantel at The Gables, High Street, (H. W. Smith) and BELOW: an early picture of The Gables; (note the advertising next door). (Ron White)

Three early George Ward photographs of the High Street.

93

ABOVE: Looking down Church Row or Alley in 1931 and
BELOW: end-on. (Staniland Pugh)

LEFT: Stiff Leadbiter's 1758 agreement with William Drake to build the new Shardeloes, and RIGHT: Samuel Maycock's June 1789 account for bricklaying at the Crown Inn for the Drake estate.
(Both County Record Office)

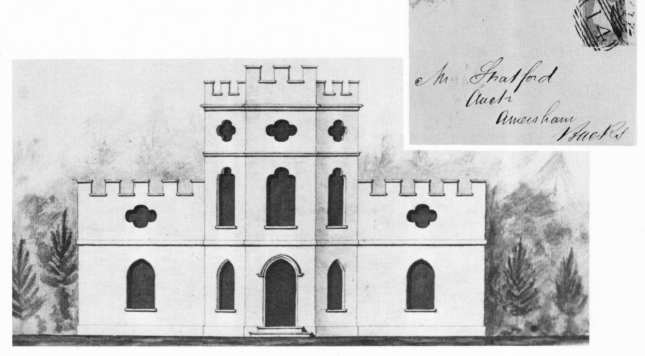

ABOVE: Shardeloes today. (Howard Son and Gooch)

RIGHT: this is the earliest known letter to an Amersham auctioneer.

BELOW: W. Lindley designed this lodge or hunting box for the Drakes in 1784. (County Record Office)

ABOVE: The railway coach called at Black Horse House, by Black Horse Bridge c1900 (J. Hearn), and BELOW: 119 High Street—'The Dungeons' which spawned a false Drake death legend.

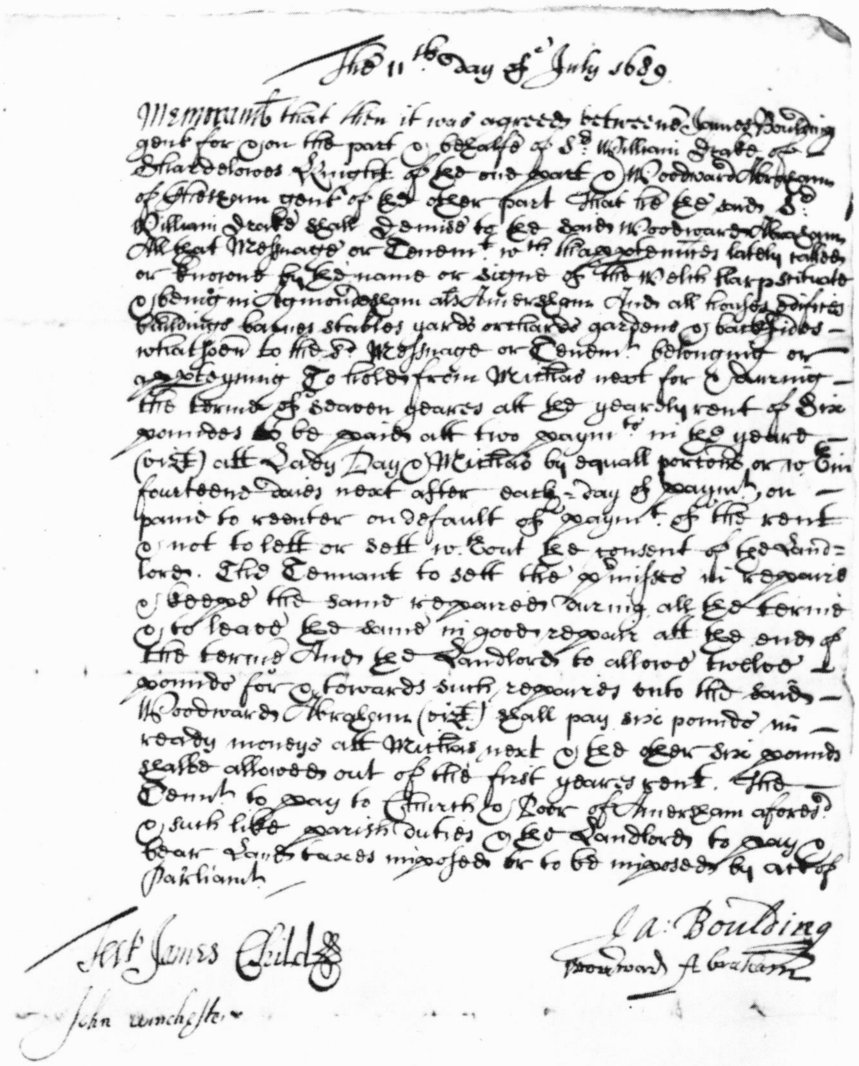

The 11th day of July 1689

Memorandum that then it was agreed betweene James Boulding gent for & on the part & behalfe of Sr William Drake of Shardelowes Knight of the one part & Woodward Abraham of Agmondesham gent of the other part that the said Sr William Drake shall demise to the said Woodward Abraham All that Messuage or Tenement wch [illegible] lately called or knowne by the name or signe of the Welsh Harp situate & being in Agmondesham als Amersham And all houses edifices buildings barnes stables yards orchards gardens & backsides whatsoever to the sd Messuage or Tenemt belonging or appertaining To hold from Michas next for & during the terme of seaven yeares att the yearely rent of Six pounds to be paid att two paymts in the yeare (vizt) att Lady Day & Michas by equall porcons or wthin fourteene daies next after each day of paymt on paine to reenter on default of paymt of the rent & not to lett or sett wthout the consent of the Land-lord. The Tenant to kepe the premisses in repaire & keepe the same repaired during all the terme & to leave the same in good repair att the end of the terme And the Landlord to allowe twelve pounds for & towards such repaires unto the said Woodward Abraham (vizt) shall pay six pounds in ready moneys att Michas next & the other six pounds shall be allowed out of the first yeares rent. The Tennt to pay to Church & Poore of Amersham aforesd & such like parish duties & the Landlords to pay all Land taxes imposed or to be imposed by act of Parliament.

Test James Childe
John Winchester

Ja: Boulding
Woodward Abraham

Local refreshment was assured on 11 July, 1689, when James Boulding signed an agreement on Sir William Drake's behalf, agreeing to let the Welsh Harp in Amersham to Woodward Abraham of Church Street, for seven years at £6 per annum (County Record Office), and BELOW: a collective thirst was doubtless engendered when the Amersham husbands played the bachelors on 25 August, 1873. Jno. Weller umpired, and the married men won by 175 runs to 112.

On the Light Side

Although the Whit Monday fair, granted in 1613, was allowed to lapse, the September fair (for which the Tyrwhitt Drakes still hold the charter rights) has been consistently maintained for more than 750 years. But it long ago lost its original purpose and use and became an amusement fair.

On 19 and 20 September each year High Street, Market Square and The Broadway (and formerly also Dovecotes Meadow) are crowded with these colourful money spinners.

With the considerable amount of traffic through Amersham (for which on these occasions only a minimum two-way width of road is left available) both the police and the local authorities have sought a way to move, or even terminate, this annual disruption. The first really determined effort was made in 1959, followed by others during subsequent years. A copy of the original charter was obtained and studied by the council's solicitor. Part of it, in translation, reads as follows:

'John, by the grace of God . . . Know ye that we have given and granted, and by this present Charter confirmed, to our dear and faithful Geoffrey, son of Peter, Earl of Essex, and his heirs after him, that they have every year one Fair at Agmondesham for two days duration, to wit in the Vigil of the Nativity of the Blessed Mary and in the day of the same Feast . . .'. This charter, dated at Marlborough on the 9 April, 1201 'in the second year of our reign' carries a margin note cancelling the original charter of the year 1200.

Such fairs were usually dated by saints' days or other distinctive events in the Christian calendar, particularly when they could be linked with the dedication of the local parish church. The church at Amersham is dedicated to St Mary; but its patronal feast day is 8 September. When this country changed to the Gregorian calendar in 1752, eleven days had to be lost between 2 and 14 September. Consequently the 8th under the 'Olde Kalendar' became the 19th.

It was found by the local authority that the Fairs Act of 1871 gave the Secretary of State the power to abolish old fairs where it could be proven that 'it would be for the convenience and advantage of the public' for such action to be taken. The procedure was for some local persons to bring a complaint before their magistrates. If these decided that a case had been made out, they could then make representation to the Secretary of State under the Act.

As an alternative to civil action, the fair organisers were approached and asked if they would agree to move to a less inconvenient location around the town; they declined. So the September Fair in its modern format still brings colour, traffic congestion, crowds of participants and spectators, blaring music and, after dark, flaring lights to Amersham for two brief days every autumn—and many people say 'Long may it do so'.

Even up to the earlier part of the present century people in small country towns such as Amersham had little amusement or entertainment, and few indeed had a holiday away from home. So the September Fair was a highlight of the year, and coupled with it in the annual calendar was the Amersham Flower Show. Originally staged by the local Odd-fellows, it was held until about seventy years ago in Dovecotes (or Duffats) Meadow which is now shared by a public car park and a County Highways depot. From then, until it lapsed shortly before the last war, the venue was the Rectory Meadow between School Lane and Rectory Hill.

The opening, on a Thursday afternoon, was heralded by the march through the town to Dovecotes of the now defunct Town Band, banner waving and musicians blowing their loudest after a final rehearsal in their wooden hut up Cherry Lane. Originally formed as the Amersham Sons of Temperance Brass Band, disbanded after some of its players broke the pledge, it was later reformed and maintained until the late 1930s. Although this was a brass band (Chesham had a silver one) during the years that George Ward was the band-master he himself played a silver cornet which he had won in a musical contest.

Now almost forgotten are the annual sprat suppers held in the Maltings in Barn Meadow. Townspeople were invited by the Wellers, sat on long forms and were served with these tasty little fish, fried on shining steel malt shovels.

Another annual event attracted far more than local interest. Horse Racing took place every Easter Monday during the latter part of the 19th century. The course was up the east side of Shardeloes Park towards Mop End. There were events for ponies, Galloways and one mile flat races; also hurdle races, jumping and driving competitions. Until 1898 there were boys' running contests of one hundred yards, quarter mile and one mile steeplechase.

The squire, T. W. T. Drake, pressed the organising committee to run the meeting in accordance with Jockey Club rules, but they declined to do so, after which he largely with-drew his supporting interest. This Easter Monday sporting occasion finally terminated after a fatal accident when a jockey fell and broke his neck. A tree, with a memorial plaque on it, was planted at the spot in the park where this tragedy occurred.

A later squire, W. W. T. Drake, trained race horses at Amersham. They were stabled at Coldmoreham and their 'gallop' was across the lower park (from near the present lodges and where the cricket pitch is now) between the lake and the mansion, and then up and round to the left. Two of the best known of the squire's horses were 'Irish Mail' and 'Walnut Tree'.

Just before the 1914/18 war the former gained second place in the Grand National. Jack Drake, the squire's son, said to be the best amateur jockey at that time, was to have ridden it, but he switched over to someone else's horse, which proved to be a racing failure. Anthony rode 'Irish Mail' at short notice, and the turf opinion was that this horse would have won if Jack Drake had ridden it.

The famous Old Berkeley Hunt used to have its hounds kennelled at Coldmoreham and a local businessman, John Brazil, has now been the Master for many years. The Boxing Day meet is held at Mantles Green. The 17th century half-timbered 'Huntsman's Cottage' in The Broadway retains its name from the time when it was occupied by the Hunt whipper-in.

Amersham Cricket Club was founded about 1856 by William Bright, William Aldridge and the Revd E. T. Drake who was a member of the MCC and, according to Lillywhite's 'Guide to Cricketers', a 'magnificent hitter, splendid field and first rate slow underhand bowler'. This sporting parson, Rector of Amersham for forty years, was also captain of this club until 1904. They played in Hand Meadow at Shardeloes until 1886 when they shifted to Barn Meadow. In 1905 they returned to Shardeloes but were again in Barn Meadow three years later, remaining there until 1929 when they finally settled permanently back on their present ground at Shardeloes.

A second (Thursday) team was formed by A. H. Haddon, the chemist, for shopkeepers and others who were not able to play at the week-end, with Mr Haddon as captain until 1910.

An early 'domestic' match was held between marrieds and singles in 1873, the former winning by 63 runs. Dr J. C. Gardner, that well known all round sportsman, was chairman of the club for nearly forty years, and captain from 1905, followed in 1914 by Rev C. E. Briggs who succeeded Rev E. T. Drake as Rector. He was replaced in 1929 by H. R. Hoare.

The June Cricket Week, started in 1930, became a popular annual event. At least two of the club's members were subsequently capped for Bucks County and one became a Cambridge cricket Blue.

Amersham Town Football Club originally held its home matches in Barn Meadow, by permission of the Brewery Company which then owned it, and used the Church School across the lane for changing. They played in the Chesham League, the Chesham Charity and the Aylesbury League, winning all three cups in the 1910/11 season, whilst their excellent performances a few years later enabled them to bring home a total of five cups for the season.

With the advice and support of Dr J. C. Gardner, they moved to their present ground at Spratley's Meadow in 1923; the kick-off for the first match there was by a small girl— the squire's eldest daughter. Their first permanent buildings and stand were erected in the 1930s, and these have since been improved and extended.

Amersham had its own swimming pool some three-quarters of a century ago. Known as the 'Upper', it was on the little River Misbourne at the west end of the town, beyond the mill. Varying in depth from about two to nearly five feet, it had a mainly gravel bed, although it used to get muddy in the shallows where the children played; the stream kept it clean. High diving was practised by the more venturesome boys from the tops of the adjoining willow trees. Here Jack Archer would be watched admiringly by others as he dived in and then swam the full length of the pool under water with his eyes wide open.

Originally this bathing and swimming place was screened from the road and at each end by corrugated iron sheeting, with the further side separated from Spratley's Meadow only by an open palisading. But in the early 1920s, the Parish Council fully enclosed it. They also provided wooden staging and seats, and hooks for clothing; there was a little wooden bridge across each end of the pool. Some keen townspeople, such as Fred Fuller, used this pool daily, summer and winter; but by about 1930 it was falling out of use, and the site was finally cleared soon after the end of the last war.

For well over a decade Amersham had the distinction of possessing its own quite successful theatre. This was after another repertory theatre had been run for a few years in the Elizabethan barn of Bois Farm, which is now part of the Beacon School in Chesham Bois. The former 'Playbox' cinema (originally the Bijou Hall) was taken over, renamed the 'Playhouse' and opened by Sally Latimer with Noel Coward's 'Hay Fever' on Boxing Day evening in 1936. The weather was cold and foggy as the cast, huddling around a small oil stove, made-up in front of a broken mirror by the light of one bare electric bulb.

With producer Caryl Jenner joining the company two years later, a considerable reputation built up through well over twenty seasons, during which time more than five hundred plays, each of one week's duration, were produced and enthusiastically applauded by the keen audiences. The seating capacity was just 240. Although support was basically local, many regular attenders came from further away, and during the war years the audiences were much augmented by evacuees. Quite a few of those acting here later became well known on stage and screen and through radio and television, especially Dirk Bogarde.

In the post-war years conditions became difficult. Sally Latimer and Caryl Jenner were succeeded by Mr and Mrs Ferris, who already had associations with the theatre, but they also failed to sustain repertory in Amersham. Sarah Churchill and her husband Vic Oliver considered taking over, but finally decided against it. In 1956 a local estate agent acquired the property, froze its use while local people considered ways of resurrecting the theatre, and when it was obvious this was economically impractical, turned it into auction rooms.

ABOVE: The horse was a means to sport as well as work: The Old Berkeley Hunt, a picture presented to Capt T. D. Tyrwhitt-Drake in 1894 by the Hunt followers (Amersham Town Council), and BELOW: the Horse Racing Committee of c1900. (L. Haddon)

ABOVE: Amersham Brass Band in 1910, with bandmaster George Ward standing on the right with his silver cornet, and BELOW: when he took up his camera for the Coronation festivities in 1911. (Ron White)

103

ABOVE LEFT: Amersham Town FC 1910/11, and CENTRE: the eldest
Drake daughter kicks off for the first match at Spratley's meadow.
(L. Haddon)

BELOW LEFT: Once the Amersham Repertory Theatre, now an auction room, with CENTRE: Sally Latimer and Caryl Jenner, dramatic pioneers there.

ABOVE RIGHT: The Regent Cinema, (Regent Buildings) opened 2 December, 1928 (and closed in the fifties), with BELOW: the men who built it for Woodley's. (Jack Reading)

ABOVE: Woodside Farm—the old barn, now part of
BELOW: the Community Centre, in Chiltern Avenue.

106

Good Neighbours

Cherry Lane winds steeply southwards from High Street to nearly 550 feet above sea-level. Amongst trees and floral gardens between this lane and the main road to Wycombe is the Chilterns Crematorium, opened in 1966. Further up the lane lies the secluded hamlet of Woodrow (from 'wuda raw' meaning a lane through a wood) with its pretty brick and timbered cottages, including the former school house. Set in well wooded grounds noted for their rare specimen trees, Woodrow High House was built in 1656, and for a while, home to Oliver Cromwell's family, now the training headquarters of the London Federation of Boys' Clubs.

This hamlet is included in the civil parish of Amersham, as is most of Winchmore Hill (the name derived from the Old English for a boundary hill) reached by a now largely built-up lane beyond the 'Queen's Head'. Opposite here, on a site still called Whielden Gate, one of the last toll houses stood until the 1920s. The 18th century turnpike road was constructed by the wealthy Cecil family, Marquesses of Salisbury, from their seat at Hatfield to join the London-Bath road between Marlow and Reading. They were all afflicted with gout and had to make frequent journeys to take the waters at the spa in Bath. Set around Winchmore Hill's extensive and sloping common are more of the typical local brick and flint cottages. Below the chair factory, The Row is a long hillside terrace of 17th century cottages where most of the pottery workers once lived.

Coleshill, beyond Amersham, off Gore Hill, occupies the highest location in the immediate district; the name comes from 'kolle', a head or hilltop. In this long village, centred on a 'Y' following a dog-leg, many cottages, some handsome Georgian residences, and Tudor and later farmhouses survive. In 1649 there were forty families in Coleshill, and 200 persons. Blaeu's map of Bucks shows 'Colshull' as 'Part of Hardford Shire', and so it remained until after 1832. Its detachment is commemorated by the handsome Georgian residence south of the village, Hertfordshire House.

The original Coleshill manor house is now the modernised Stock Place. Here in 1606 the poet, Edmund Waller was born, cousin of both John Hampden and Oliver Cromwell. He sat as one of the MPs for Amersham in Charles II's parliaments, having already sat for Chepping Wycombe when it was claimed that he was the youngest ever MP at the age of sixteen.

Opposite the common, beyond the high-set village pond which has never dried up since 1921 is the now sail-less brick windmill built by Thomas Grove in 1856. Although refronted, the former 'Fleur-de-lys' inn dates in part from the 15th century. When it was modernised after the last war the first two figures of a date '16 . . .' were found carved on one of the massive roof timbers. It is known to have been occupied from about the year 1700 by William Bunce, a potter, who had his kiln close by. Prisoners of the Napoleonic war were possibly billeted here. French writing, executed in candle smoke, once embellished the plastering of an upper room. Unfortunately the plaster was too perished for the writing to be preserved. Early 19th century French coins were also found here, and others have been picked up around the village.

Although Chesham Bois adjoins Amersham-on-the-Hill, its earlier associations were with Great Chesham. The partly wooded common survives from the once vast expanse which stretched from Hyde Heath to Little Chalfont. The parish church, in a secluded position away from the village, has evolved from the 13th century chapel of the former manor house which was for so long occupied by the Cheyne family. Although now a residential area, Chesham Bois was formerly woodlands with four farms, and a mill recorded in Domesday but since rebuilt. Mayhall and Ivy House, with their period dwellings, are still maintained as farms; but all that remains of Bois Farm is the splendid Elizabethan barn, now part of the Beacon School, whilst the main dwelling of Manor Farm (renamed Manor House) has been largely rebuilt and enlarged, and its farm workers' cottages along North Road converted into private houses, as has the original brick and flint school on the corner of Chestnut Lane.

LEFT: Coleshill windmill, when it still had its sails, and RIGHT: the doorway
to Coleshill School; the bricks are furrowed where the pupils sharpened
their slate pencils.

108

ABOVE: Hertfordshire House, Coleshill; RIGHT: a 15th century gilded crucifix from the village (County Museum), and BELOW: Stock Place as it is today—once home of Edmund Waller.

109

Sir

*This is to Inform you that
I have Bought woodrow farm at
£2900 — and have Paid Mr Mallors one
Hundred Pounds in part of Payment with
I Recd of Mr Eeles Mr Marshall has made
the agreement with is Sind
If Mr Allen Leaves wood Row farm Mr Complin
wishes to Takes it if it meets with your
Approbation*

I am Sir your Obt Servt

Amersham 15 June 1802   *John Croft*

To be SOLD by AUCTION,
By SAMUEL MARTIN,
On the PREMISES,

On MONDAY the 29th Day of AUGUST, 1774,

(Precisely at TWELVE o'Clock at Noon)

IN THREE LOTS.

Lot I. A Valuable COPYHOLD ESTATE, confisting of a modern new-built Brick Manfion-Houfe, known by the Name of HIGH-HOUSE, in a moft agreeable and elevated Situation, on WYCOMB-HEATH, in BUCKS, 28 Miles from London, 1 Mile from Amerfham, 4 Miles from Wycomb, 14 Miles from Aylesbury, 9 Miles from Watford, and near a Turnpike-Road; being a healthy Spot, on a gravelly Soil, commanding various extenfive Profpects; and is in a fine fporting Country, abounding with Plenty of Game.

HIGH-HOUSE is a fubftantial Dwelling, in the moft compleat Repair, elegantly fitted up for immediate Reception: Contains four Rooms, with Dreffing-Rooms and Clofets, on each Floor; three Stories high; together with a large light Kitchen, back Kitchen, Dairy, Pantry, Wafh-Houfe, Butler's-Room, good Cellaring, and other convenient Offices: detached are two Coach-Houfes, two Stables for nine Horfes, a paved Yard, a Grainery, a Dove-Houfe, Brew-Houfe, and many convenient Out-Offices; furrounded with three Gardens, an Orchard, and Pleafure-Ground, well cropp'd and ftock'd with all Kinds of Wall and other Fruit Trees, now in their greateft Perfection: With two Fifh-Ponds of Carp, Tench, and Gold Fifh.

The Whole of which Premifes contain about five Acres of Land, more or lefs; and have an unlimited Right to a fine extenfive Common.

N. B. The Purchafer of this Lot may, if agreeable, buy all the Houfhold Furniture, which is elegant and almoft new, at a fair Valuation; otherwife it will be fold, as advertifed.

Lot II. A FREEHOLD and COPYHOLD ESTATE, confifting of a Farm, near Lot I, with a Dwelling-Houfe, two Barns, Stabling, and other Out-Houfes; with a Cottage, Garden, Yard, &c. containing about Forty Acres, more or lefs, of Pafture and Arable Land, in the fineft Order; is Tithe-free, and has an unlimited Right of Commonage.

Lot III. A FREEHOLD ESTATE, confifting of a Farm, adjoining to Lot II, with a good Dwelling-Houfe, Barn, Stable, and other Out-Houfes, Orchard, Yard, &c. together with about Forty Acres, more or lefs, of Arable, Pafture and Wood Land, all adjoining. The Land is in

LEFT: In 1802 John Croft advised Squire Drake that he had bought Woodrow Farm for £2,900, and BELOW: Auction announcement in 1774 of the sale of Woodrow High House.
(Documents from County Record Office)

ABOVE: The Row, Winchmore Hill, where the potters lived.

BELOW: The original Chesham Bois school and
mistress's house built in 1846.

ABOVE: The 19th century Chesham Bois village bakery, Fern Cottage, North Road, and BELOW: Chesham Bois Vicar, Rev G. H. Lawrence on his rounds in the 1920s.

The Haunting Past

In spite of Amersham's antiquity, few instances of ghostly or other strange manifestations have been recorded, the most persistent being the Green Lady of Woodrow (Lady Helena Stanhope) who is still allegedly seen at intervals. Local legends feature subterranean passages, such as one supposedly from Shardeloes, under the lake to somewhere on the opposite side of the valley; or another which was supposed to run from The Gables in High Street to the parish church. The former possibly had its origin in a semi-tunnel entrance found near the mansion, which may well have been used to transport wine and bulk household goods into the network of cellars still beneath it. The origin of the tunnel from The Gables can be traced to the centre of this Tudor building, where the staircase is supported above a brick vaulting which looks like a tunnel entrance, but has been investigated and found to be only a wine cellar. A similar construction feature can be seen at Tresco House a few doors further up the street.

Another story connected with The Gables, and due no doubt to the fact that it had once belonged to Missenden Abbey, featured the nun's grave. Oddly enough, some years ago when the rear courtyard paving was relaid, bones said to be human were found there. Although the actual houses are best not named, there have been instances from time to time of so-called hauntings, usually manifested by a sensation of acute coldness, irrespective of the weather; generally this was found to be in one particular room, but sometimes in various parts of the house. However, all these would appear to have been exorcised successfully by the time honoured process of 'bell, book and candle'.

Amongst all the recountings of creakings, footsteps and groanings or clanking of chains which, although they may sound eerie at night are usually nothing more than the natural movements of timber-framed buildings, one such instance is not so easily explained. This was the sound of someone walking up a staircase in the side wall of a house which the occupants heard quite distinctly on various occasions in their bedroom. Although it has been proved that they were quite unaware of the fact, in the back of a deep cupboard next door against this same wall there is a length of old carved woodwork, like balustrading, half plastered over. There is no reason to think that this wall is not completely solid; but the footsteps are still being heard . . .

Ghosts traditionally refuse to be photographed, but the portraits on these three pages evoke the spirit of a bygone age, when manners, family and a proper pride in achievement, in appearance and in work were taken for granted. George Ward captured the atmosphere of the late 19th and early 20th centuries when he recorded these unknown Amersham people for posterity.

As his 'My Album' card eloquently puts it: Here I see familiar faces, Ranged together, side by side, Occupying friendship's places, Treasured with affection's pride ... Love selected, lie reflected, Lifelike on each hallowed page.

115

Metroland

Although what is now called Old Amersham in the Misbourne valley had been an established town since mediaeval days, the 'top of the hill', known as Amersham Common, did not develop until the railway came in 1892. The first buildings around the station were just below the bridge, with a few others opposite what is now the 'Iron Horse'; 144 to 158 Station Road. Like the public house, these were built by George Darlington and the terrace opposite built by Martin & Sons. The building occupied as offices by the Amersham Town Council was originally a temperance hotel. Here, too, was a sub-post office. Two houses between Oakfield Corner and South Road (11 and 49 Chesham Road) were built by William Gomm and George Pearce, together with some in Chesham Bois. In these they used window frames, fireplaces and other fittings which they bought from houses demolished in London to provide the site for Marylebone station in 1899.

Many years before that the 'Boot and Slipper' stood, with a pair of cottages beside it, on the open and windswept common which extended almost unbroken from Hyde Heath, along Copperkins Lane (where the remnants are the wide grass verges now defined as manorial waste) and on past Blackhorse Bridge almost to Bell Lane. A narrow strip of bracken from this common still persists near Grimsdells corner. The numerous public footpaths criss-crossing amongst the houses in Chestnut Lane, Chestnut Close and Parkfield Avenue, are believed to survive from the original footways across this former common.

In the 1890s, Station Road was only a cart track, and even many years later Hill Avenue was still an unmade road with posts across it at the station end and an open farm gate near Oakfield Corner. Stanley Hill was just a narrow country lane, the only road between the common and the town being Rectory Hill. This was deeply rutted from the iron shoes which had to be put under the wheels of the horse-drawn carts and waggons as they negotiated what was then a much steeper descent than it is now.

There were also some brick and slated cottages in Grimsdells Lane (formerly Meads Lane) near the corner of Short Way (originally Church Lane) and a blacksmith's forge; others were at the far end of Chestnut Lane and in Quill Hall Lane. More cottages and another inn, 'The Pheasant', were along Plantation Road and near Blackhorse Bridge where the Georgian Bridge House still stands with one of the original cottages beside it. The bridge takes its name from the flint and brick building opposite Bridge House which was originally the 'Black Horse' public house.

Up the adjoining Raans Road is Park Place (to be demolished) and formerly known as The Plantation. The land, probably with a small house already on it, was purchased from Lord Chesham by the Wellers, and here they built their new family residence, incorporating in it various fireplaces and other interior fittings which they acquired from the demolished manor house of Chesham Bois. At the far end of this same road stands Raans, one of the oldest and most historic residences in the district. Built (or more probably rebuilt) in 1540, it was extended in the early 17th century by the Proby family, whose arms are displayed above the entrance doorway.

During the latter part of the 19th and the early part of the 20th centuries a number of small villas and a few larger houses were built in Chestnut Lane (then known as Red Lion Road) where a fine period farmhouse called Woodside stood, its name later altered to The Chestnuts. Its site is now occupied by a local authority housing estate. There is an interesting suggestion that this could have been the Woodside to which the Quaker Peningtons moved and not the farmhouse of the same name which stood on what is now the Community Centre. At the far end of this lane were Quill Hall Cottage (demolished after the last war for re-development) and the still existing Quill Hall farmhouse.

In groups along White Lion Road were terraced or separate cottages, also the 17th century Reeves Farm, the historic Barkers (originally Baker's Farm), the set-back 'Pineapple', the period Bendrose House in its cherry orchards, and now hidden behind the Radiochemical Centre, The Piece. This picturesque half-timbered and dormered residence was originally a pair of 16th century cottages, converted and extended in later times. It retains its inglenook fireplaces and an old faggot oven. There is a tradition that it was an inn during the 17th century. Nearby, on the corner of Finch Lane, stands the modernised Georgian 'White Lion', and down this lane are some attractive cottages leading to what remains of Hovel Farm. The modern Roman Catholic Church is set within the drive gateway of the secluded Georgian and Regency Beel House. This was occupied by the Lyle family of Tate & Lyle in the early part of the present century and was later the home of the film actor, Dirk Bogarde until he moved when the Girls' High School was built. Beel is a corruption of beadle and would therefore appear to have been the house of the bailiff or parish officer. Similarly the origin of Reeves suggests this had been occupied by the reeve who was appointed to safeguard the interests of the tenants of the manorial lord in feudal days.

From this end of White Lion Road the district, although still part of Amersham, is known as Little Chalfont, a name given to it by a property developer between the last two wars. Formerly it was all farmland, mainly belonging to Oldhouse Farm across the railway to the north, Lodge Farm to the east, Loudhams Farm on the corner of Burtons Lane, and southwards Snells Farm, Burtons Farm and Cokes Farm. Cokes Farm was recorded as Cokeyes in the 15th century, and is now, like Loudhams an attractive period residence, with a splendid contemporary barn. In its orchard is the tomb of the members of the Grimsdell family who died between 1647 and 1739.

Little Chalfont, with the convenience of its own railway station (formerly called Chalfont Road station) and its modern parades of shops, village hall, sports club ground, schools, churches and new public recreation ground, has attracted a vastly increased population during the last quarter of a century, largely represented by commuters.

Similarly at Amersham-on-the-Hill, earlier residential development began within easy reach of the railway station in what was to become widely publicised as Metroland. At first mainly smaller houses were built, detached and often in cottage style, or in gabled semi-detachment, as in Rickmansworth Road (erected by Martin & Sons), Grimsdells Lane, New Road and Lexham Gardens.

The builder's yard of Alfred Woodley Ltd, in Lexham Gardens has an interesting association. Louis Tussaud, one of the great grandsons of the celebrated Madame Tussaud, broke away from the family establishment in Baker Street, and it was in the carpenters' shop here that, with a girl assistant, he started to make his own waxworks. He set up an exhibition in Regent Street which was destroyed in a fire. He then began another at Brighton, this

Amersham building firm providing the staging for the displays; but it did not prove a financial success. So it was removed to the first of the Butlin holiday camps at Skegness, Woodleys again carrying out the necessary work. Here, too, it proved unsuccessful. There is still a Louis Tussaud waxworks at Brighton but under different and successful ownership.

In 1863 the population of Amersham was 3,019. At the 1911 census it had increased only to 3,392 but the 1931 census figure was 6,121 which had nearly doubled at the 1951 census to 11,205. The estimated population of the whole civil parish in 1975 was approximately 17,000.

During the earlier part of the present century Amersham became known for its race of six-toed cats which appear to have originated at the 'Griffin'. Only a few years ago a letter came to the local authority from someone in the United States asking if these particular cats still existed. One was found of advanced years and the reassuring reply sent to America. Amersham seems to have specialised in unusual feline varieties, for it also produced a strain of bob-tailed cats (not Manx, which have no tail at all, but like the old Cornish bob-tail) and these can still be seen around, generally in the vicinity of Whielden Street.

Numerous houses, many of them quite large, were built at Amersham-on-the-Hill after the 1914/18 war; along Copperkins Lane, Chesham Road, Hervines Road, the further part of Sycamore Road, Highland Road, Parkfield Avenue, South Road and elsewhere. When in the early 1930s, the Metropolitan Railway Company bought up large areas of farmland and engaged contractors to build reasonably priced detached and semi-detached houses in new roads and closes, people who had already come to know Amersham and the surrounding Chiltern countryside through the Metroland walks leaflets, were not slow to come to live in The Drive, The Rise, Woodside Close, Green Lane, Woodside Road, Highfield Close and Grimsdells Lane. Of the former farmhouses, Hyrons, a finely timbered but partly rebuilt residence, still stands in Hyrons Lane where its former farm bridge over to Highlands Road is at the highest point on the whole of the old Great Central Railway system; but the farmhouse of Woodside has now been demolished although its barns and outbuildings were repaired and preserved to form the first part of the modern Community Centre.

Also in the early 1930s, other building firms were busy expanding this Metropolitan Railway commuter district, and the local authority developed Council housing eastwards from New Road, also in Old Amersham along School Lane and off Gore Hill, and later at Pondwicks where the pond had earlier been filled in with the surplus excavated soil when Darlingtons had laid the main sewer through the town. Gradually, too, the long maintained 'break' between the original town in the valley and the development over the former common was filled in with the housing on the Hundred Acres estate, in Station Road, First Avenue, Chequers Hill and Stanley Hill which was then the main road from Rickmansworth to Amersham.

In 1929 a controversial residence was built on the slope above the modern Station Road houses. Called High-and-Over, designed for Prof Bernard Ashmole by Amyas Douglas Connell, this was a completely new idiom for England, on the principles of Le Corbusier, the famous Swiss-French architect, and it became the prototype for many such concrete and glass houses in other places. Three years later it 'spawned' four much smaller houses in the same style up the steep road to the High-and-Over entry lodge. The concrete mushroom water tower above the main residence (for there was no company water supply) became a much criticised hilltop landmark.

With the steady increase in population, more shops were required at Amersham-on-the-Hill in addition to the few just below the station. So the right-hand side of Hill Avenue became largely retail shops, with others which had been built around Oakfield Corner into Chesham Road about 1910. A beginning was made on the present main shopping centre in Sycamore Road, extended during the 1930s with others at Sycamore Corner and more along Woodside Road. Often existing private houses were bought up and converted into shops or had lock-ups built in front of them. Later the central parade on the left-hand side of Sycamore Road was erected on the site of what had been a large private house and orchard, with Sainsbury's and Boots occupying the prime positions. Further along, Lipton's supermarket occupies the site of the once large and well equipped cinema which was opened in 1928; but with changing conditions, this had to be closed down and demolished.

During the last twenty-five years, and particularly since the complete electrification of the railway in 1961, there has been much further residential, commercial and office development, and various redevelopments, the erection of blocks of flats in all parts of Amersham-on-the-Hill, and the rather unfortunate complex of Council flats in White Lion Road. In Old Amersham which, until then, had remained almost entirely untouched, some new houses were built and many of the cottages were modernised and often considerably enlarged. Commercially, too, a great change has now occurred in the character of this ancient and picturesque town. Whereas at the end of the last war there were about a score of general stores and other food and utility shops, by 1975 nearly all of these had become antique showrooms, picture galleries or gift and craft shops; there is now also a silversmith. They attract probably even greater numbers of visitors and tourists than the historic buildings of the town. So breaking a habit of many generations, old residents have to do most of their shopping 'up the Hill'.

The centre, but perhaps not the true heart of Amersham is now between Woodside Road and the railway with its complex of contemporary buildings—halls, swimming pool, legal courts, police building, health centre and public library, with future planning for an administrative block to accommodate the Chiltern District Council. The large glazed building which adjoins the recreation ground comprising the international sized pool, learners' pool, spectators' gallery, excellent changing accommodation and sun-bathing patio on the south side, is indeed a far cry from the primitive little pool made on the Misbourne for the keen members of the former Cygnet Swimming Club!

The civil parish of Amersham covers 6,451 acres, or just over 10 square miles; but although largely built up, it still includes a considerable area of characteristic Chiltern countryside; hills, valleys and woods. There are approximately seventy defined public footpaths in the parish of Amersham totalling some 30 miles.

For visitors and residents also, there are the public open spaces. The first recreation ground was the five acres Barn Meadow, between High Street and School Lane, bordered on the south by the course of the little River Misbourne. Later a recreation ground was acquired at Amersham-on-the-Hill behind the present Grammar School. When the opportunity came to purchase Hervines Park in the early 1930s, this much smaller open space became part of the school playing fields. Situated at the far end of Hervines Road, the fine park of 28½ acres includes a plantation of mixed larch and beech with a few oaks above the railway cutting, linked by an avenue of fir trees and newly planted cherries and various hardwoods to Hervines Road, and an area of mature beech woodland beneath which bluebells provide a scented carpet in springtime. The open part of this park had to be ploughed up for crops during the last war but has been restored to provide an extensive level expanse of grassland with games pitches and a bowling green.

Under the King George VI Playing Field scheme, a further recreation ground of four acres was purchased off Woodside Road and appropriately named King George's Field. Since then provision for recreational activities has had to be made for the eastern part of the parish. An area of about two acres is leased in White Lion Road, and 18½ acres have been purchased at Little Chalfont with views over the Chess valley.

The attractive Memorial Gardens in The Broadway were laid out as a setting for the town's war memorial. A few years ago the disused allotments of Church Mead, between here and the Misbourne, were acquired to provide a riverside addition with paths and seats. The adjoining churchyard, now closed for burials, has been handed over to the Town Council.

In 1976 Mop End marsh, an area of about half-an-acre owned by the Central Electricity Generating Board, was reclaimed to be used by the children of local schools as a nature study site. The removal of dead timber and some clearance of reeds and silt has provided water and marshland with much interesting flora and fauna.

Closely associated with the life of Amersham is the little River Misbourne, the course of which lies behind the houses on the north side of the town. Its name is of Celtic derivation, being originally Mease, meaning a stream. In Saxon days it was known as the Messebourne. Until fairly recent times it provided the power for the Amersham water mills. Like all chalk streams, its flow is intermittent, and there is a tradition that the drying up of the Misbourne always presages some national or world disaster, which, quite by chance it has sometimes done, as in 1914 and 1939. It was even featured in the Continental press in 1951 when 'Le Monde' published an article headed: 'La Misbourne Coule de Nouveau: Signe de Paix' (The Misbourne flows anew: Omen of peace). During the much colder weather of the late 19th century, people used to skate right down the Misbourne to Uxbridge.

Originally it rose right up in the Hampden country; but by the 1930s, its source was just the other side of Great Missenden, and now its course is even shorter. This is largely due to the vastly increased amount of water withdrawn from the deep chalk by boreholes for present-day requirements. Yet when the visible bed of this little feeder of the Thames is quite dry (as it now so often is) it has been found by geological survey that the water is still flowing strongly in a lower river bed. So the river which attracted Amersham's first inhabitants still flows, nearly 2,000 years later, a silver thread which links the town with its origins.

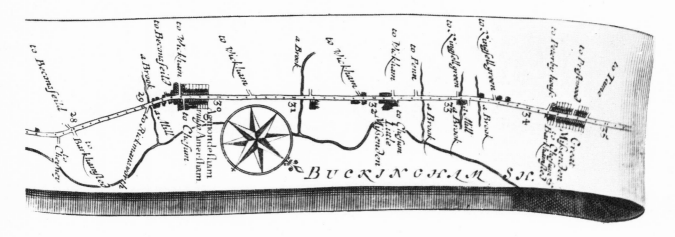

Amersham was on the London-Aylesbury Road in 1675 in John Ogilby's strip map—a place between other places.

ABOVE: By 1912, traffic thundering down the broad High Street necessitated pedestrian crossings—to escape the filth in the road. The cobbled lines can be seen in front of each right hand equipage. (L. Haddon); LEFT: some attempt was made to clear up the consequences of equine power, and RIGHT: this did not stop the dreadful conditions when the weather was bad.

ABOVE: A landmark long before Amersham's hilltop development—the
Boot and Slipper, Rickmansworth Road/Chesham Road junction, and
BELOW: an even earlier landmark—the impressive barn at Cokes Farm,
Little Chalfont.

INSET: The toll-house at Whielden Gate opposite the Queens Arms on the
Cecil turnpike.

ABOVE: The Grimsdell tombstone near Cokes Farm, and
BELOW: The Piece, White Lion Road.

124

ABOVE: Beel House, Amersham Common, and BELOW: Rectory Woods
before the railway came. (Ron White)

In 1891 they came to lay the railway and changed the face of the town; ABOVE: The 'Henry Appleby', and BELOW: the 'Calden' at Amersham on 3 October, 1891 (Both Ron White), with INSET: George Stephenson, the man behind the local transport revolution. (Mansell Collection)

WHY NOT LIVE IN METRO-LAND?

HAVE you ever realised the joy of living in the country; the pleasure of rural surroundings and bracing air? Have you ever thought of the advantages to be gained; the economies to be effected; how quickly " London's streaming roar " can be left far behind?

In Metro-land—London's nearest countryside—you will find all you can reasonably ask. It has character and charm; variety and interest. There are houses ready to live in and building land ripe for development. The train service is unrivalled; the Season Ticket Rates are low; the opportunities for outdoor sport are unlimited, whilst for health it would be hard to equal, impossible to excel.

Why not learn more about Metro-land—about its wonderful Train Service and its rapid residential development? A postcard addressed to the Commercial Manager, Metropolitan Railway, Baker Street Station, N.W.1, will bring you full information by return.

ABOVE: Early days at Amersham Station (note the milk churns), and BELOW: the Metropolitan Railway steam-drawn train at Chalfont and Latimer Station on 12 May, 1934 (Both Ron White), with RIGHT: the inside back cover of the Met's No 4 Country Walks leaflet—making claims that have not altogether stood the test of time! (E. N. Corns)

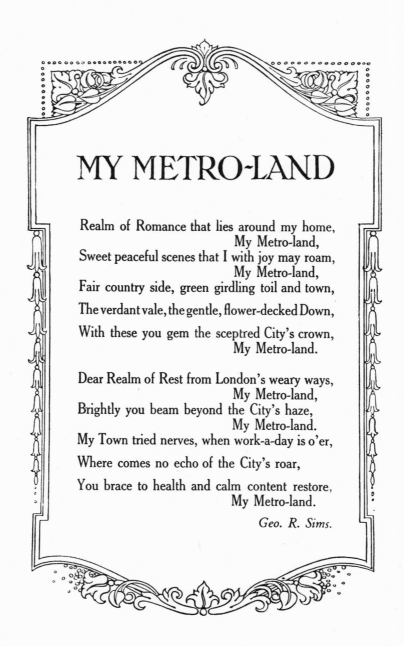

MY METRO-LAND

Realm of Romance that lies around my home,
　　　　　My Metro-land,
Sweet peaceful scenes that I with joy may roam,
　　　　　My Metro-land,
Fair country side, green girdling toil and town,

The verdant vale, the gentle, flower-decked Down,

With these you gem the sceptred City's crown,
　　　　　My Metro-land.

Dear Realm of Rest from London's weary ways,
　　　　　My Metro-land,
Brightly you beam beyond the City's haze,
　　　　　My Metro-land.
My Town tried nerves, when work-a-day is o'er,

Where comes no echo of the City's roar,

You brace to health and calm content restore,
　　　　　My Metro-land.

Geo. R. Sims.

The Met also issued the leaflet in which this paean of poetic praise was
published. (E. N. Corns)

METRO-LAND

PRICE TWO-PENCE

The front cover of another Metro-land leaflet captures exactly the appeal
of Amersham for the Londoner.

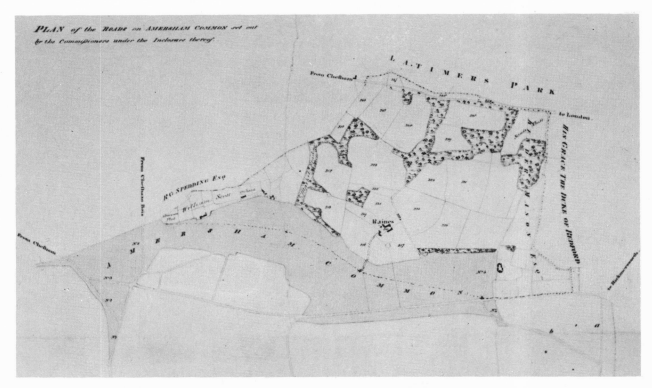

ABOVE: This plan of the enclosure of Amersham Common in 1817 contrasts
sharply with today's on-the-ground development (County Record Office),
and BELOW: so does this aerial photograph of Oakfield Corner, c1920.
(Brig E. E. F. Baker)

130

ABOVE: Amersham early this century; with CENTRE: South Road—
Chestnut Lane corner with the Punch Tree in 1912 (J. Hearn), and
BELOW: Station Road with Batchelor's Wood on the left, *c*1913.
(A. Mead)

ABOVE: Chiltern Avenue, with Woodside Road beyond the
gate; earlier this century. (Staniland Pugh)

BELOW: High and Over shocked local residents with its architectural
immodesty; these white cube houses soon joined it. Even this relatively
modern house cannot now be seen except in close-up, due to the growth
of surrounding trees.

LEFT: The Market Hall is a silent witness to yet further transport advances
—an early motorcycle in High Street (Ron White), and RIGHT: the 'Pride
of Bucks', Amersham Bus Co's charabanc (L. Haddon), and BELOW:
Stanley Hill Avenue and the footpath running off it together follow a line
laid down by Roman engineers nearly 2,000 years ago.

ABOVE : Sycamore Road seems tranquil enough in the '30s, though BELOW :
this modern picture of the other end of the street belies the hustle of a busy
shopping day—it was taken on Sunday.

ABOVE: Oakfield Corner in 1976, and BELOW: Hill Avenue, both emphasising the Metroland mode in Chilternesque architecture.

135

ABOVE LEFT: George Ward's panorama of early 20th century Amersham
evidenced things to come: the gasworks and the brewery vie with the
Parish Church for prominence, while CENTRE: Little Chalfont gradually
marches into the fields above the Latimer valley in 1976, and BELOW:
the view from the new nurses' home at Amersham Hospital might make us
grateful that the railway did not come down the hill.

ABOVE RIGHT: Even so, development has not by-passed Amersham Town itself, and BELOW: Gore Hill has had to change its course, leaving this 'cut' where the road wound downhill not so long ago.

137

Amersham Hospital Nurses' Home points up the conflict between need and desire: a necessary home for some of the community's hardest working residents, but a building out of character with its context.

John Armistead sees Amersham 1976 as perhaps George Ward might have done—through an arch darkly. Here is all the contrast between yesterday's elegance and today's transience: the handsome High Street and the cancerous motorcar—viewed from the Market Hall.

Bibliography

and further reading

Shardeloes Papers by G. Eland (Oxford University Press)
Romance of Pillow Lace by Thomas Wright
Roman Roads S.E. Midlands by The Viatores (Gollancz)
Kelly's Directory of Buckinghamshire (1907)
Dutton Allen's Directory of Oxon, Bucks & Berks (1843)
History of Amersham by—Goss of Chesham Bois (privately published)
Cricket in the Meadow by G. Quin (privately published)
Buildings of Buckinghamshire by N. Pevsner
Early Man in South Bucks by J. F. Head (J. Wright & Sons)
History of Chesham Bois by L. Elgar Pike (privately published)
History of Chair Making in High Wycombe by L. J. Mayes (Routledge)
Itinerary of John Leland edited by L. T. Smith (Centaur Press)
Oxford Dictionary of English Place Names (1936)
Chiltern District Official Handbook by L. Elgar Pike (1975)
Making of English Landscape by W. G. Hoskins (Hodder & Stoughton)
Richard Totell—His Life and Work by H. J. Byrom
Records of Buckinghamshire, 1862 to date
Victoria County History
Bucks Constabulary Centenary 1857-1957 by Alfred G. Hailstone
Political Change & Continuity 1760-1885 by Richard W. Davis (David & Charles)
The Book of Chesham by Clive Birch
Other sources:
Muniments Room, Buckinghamshire Archaeological Society
County Record Office
Buckinghamshire County Museum
County of Buckingham, Calendar to the Sessions Records, 1678-1712
Parish Churchwardens' & Overseers' Accounts

142

Subscribers

Presentation copies

1 **Amersham Town Council**
2 **Chiltern District Council**
3 **The Amersham Society**
4 **Bucks County Council**
5 **Amersham Library**
6 **The Rt. Hon. The Earl Howe, CBE, DL**
7 **Brig. E. E. F. Baker, CB, CBE, DSO, MC**

8	L. Elgar Pike	59	G. R. North	117	Mr & Mrs B. Rushbridge	163	Mrs A. R. Townsend
9	Clive Birch	60	C. T. Covell	118	J. R. Jones	164	R. Ayres
10	Gill Griffin	61	R. G. Selwyn	119	K. E. Hall	165	J. M. Allen
11	David J. Godwin	62	L. C. Cooper	120	C. W. Warden	166	Lt Col James L. Massey, JR
12	Miss Teresa Cotterell	63	Miss V. Grayson	121	Colin Robinson	167	Mrs P. A. Liechti
13	P. Edwards	64	C. J. Munton	122	Miss Joan Wadge	168	A. J. Neville
14	A. I. Woodward	65	R. A. Elsworth	123	Mrs D. Wingrove	169	R. F. East
15	Alan E. Philpott	66	J. Morton	124	Mr & Mrs J. Spalding	170	Lesley M. Seiler
16	Mrs M. Shaw	67	Miss G. Barlow	125	R. G. Newall	171	R. C. Walker
17	L. G. Pierson	68	Ann & John L. Flood	126	A. G. Parmee	172	S. Pass
18	P. G. Haynes	69	J. M. Allday	127	Mrs D. Bewers	173	Mrs Barbara Gotch
19	A. H. Roberts	70	Bucks County Library	128	Mrs M. Walshe	174 } 179 }	Maurice R. Brown
20	S. W. Grove	71	S. Hitchen	129	Mrs A. D. King		
21	P. D. Thomas	72	M. E. Tagent	130	Raans C. S. School	180	Captain S. L. Mee
22	Mrs P. I. Brackley	73	R. J. K. Turner	131	Mr & Mrs L. D. Doncaster	181	Dr G. P. Daw
23	G. A. A. Moir	74	P. Turner			182	E. L. Stredder
24	David M. Glover	75	D. Turner	132	P. J. Sharman	183	D. J. Bevis
25	M. W. Puzey	76	L. B. Aldous	133	J. E. Camp	184	Margaret R. Kenzie
26	Mrs R. J. Parsons	77	G. A. Davies	134	Carolyn Mélières	185	Jean Evans
27	J. N. Billington	78	Mrs M. New	135	Rosemary White	186	Miss K. G. G. Thompson
28	Mrs B. M. Watkins	79	G. A. Todd	136	Mrs Jean Avogadri		
29	Mr & Mrs D. M. Muncaster	80	P. D. Filsell	137	Mrs S. M. Taggart	187	Neil Bibby
		81	P. A. Hilton	138	E. P. Morris	188	Mrs F. Symonds
30	Mrs M. Mackay	82 } 92 }	Bucks County Library	139	Mrs B. Swire Griffiths	189	Mrs A. M. Arthurton
31	A. F. C. Williams			140	G. Dean	190	Mrs D. L. Bertram
32	Miss V. A. Sheen	93	C. J. Maston	141	G. A. Peiser	191	Jean B. Ladlay
33	Frank Peers	94	Mrs C. Summers	142	R. C. Watson	192	Peter Lawson
34	Reginald A. Restall	95	J. H. Leigh	143	A. J. Welch	193	Mr & Mrs P. Wardman
35	B. S. Cooper	96	L. T. Thurlby	144	H. E. Hill	194	Mr & Mrs D. D. Unwin
36	A. F. Ghysens	97	Mr & Mrs A. O. Holloway	145	B. S. Denton	195	Mr & Mrs M. T. Anderson
37	C. Chant			146	Mr & Mrs Bernard Edwards		
38	Mrs B. J. Hutchison	98	Miss F. G. Dudley-Dwight			196	Mr & Mrs Hearn
39	I. M. Bullock			147	C. A. Feather	197	Miss Joy M. Stacey
40	Mrs D. N. Fogden	99	C. J. Mallinson	148	Mrs. C. J. Brooks	198	Jane & Colin Winsborrow
41	Mrs Hilary N. Oxlade	100	Mrs Joan A. Heal	149	Mrs S. L. Stevens		
42	Miss M. Maclerie	101	Miss A. L. Duval	150	D. R. Seaby	199	D. Barnes
43	E. T. E. Turner	102	Mrs J. A. Spanner	151	Little Chalfont Rural Preservation Society	200	Cllr Mrs N. H. Downs
44	John Burr	103	Mrs B. H. Harper			201	Jennifer M. Jeacock
45	J. T. Bow	104	L. C. Nash	152	Mrs S. K. Upton	202	Wendy, Lynn, Tina & Sara Osman
46	Mrs Isabel Pike	105	Mrs A. Lloyd-Jones	153	J. R. Ruck Keene		
47	Mr & Mrs K. Monk	106	Philip D. Lawley	154	Mr & Mrs T. A. C. Schofield	203	A. L. Selwood
48	P. Howard Day	107	Mrs M. C. Brown			204	Miss M. E. Webb
49	Mrs Audrey Gurney	108	D. A. Gaston	155	Mr & Mrs M. Duncombe	205	Miss V. M. Pocock
50	Mrs Hunter	109	J. M. Learmont			206	Mrs Mitchell
51	D. Clements	110	C. Wood	156	Mrs Wells	207	Mrs S. R. West
52	G. Dunbar	111	Mrs J. C. Pitcher	157	Mrs E. J. Orton	208	R. J. White
53	R. Kirkman	112	P. L. J. Leder	158	Mrs H. J. Warren	209	Kim Patrick
54	R. J. Coles	113	Mr & Mrs Alan Helby	159	Mrs D. Deeley	210	Khalid Mahmood
55	D. Sladden	114	F. R. Forster	160	G. Lewis	211	L. W. Humphrey
56	E. Post	115	P. J. & R. Macken	161	A. E. Podbury	212	R. F. Walker
57	E. A. Alliott	116	Mr & Mrs K. R. Andrews	162	Miss D. F. Brown	213	Miss G. M. Mitchell
58	Howard Son & Gooch						

ENDPAPERS: Tudor wall paintings, discovered in 1931 at 56, High Street, Amersham, surrounded here by a painted decoration found in a first floor bedroom at the Crown Hotel. The paintings are within panels, of figures about four feet deep, known as the Nine Worthies; the faces suggest portraits of local people, perhaps once actors in an Elizabethan pageant. Those reproduced are ABOVE LEFT: Charlemagne; BELOW LEFT: Godfrey de Bouillon; CENTRE LEFT: Julius Caesar; CENTRE RIGHT: Duke Joshua; ABOVE RIGHT: King David; BELOW RIGHT: Hector of Troy.

BACK COVER: In 1786 an Amersham teenager made this delightful sampler.